Ismail Merchant's first film wa[...] of Women which was nomin[...] in 1961 for an Academy Award and was an official entry from the United States in the Cannes Film Festival the same year. En route to the festival Merchant met director James Ivory and they agreed to form a partnership, Merchant Ivory Productions, to make English language theatrical features in India for the international market. For the past thirty-five years, Merchant Ivory Productions has endured as one of the most productive collaborations in cinema, bringing forth such films as *Shakespeare Wallah, The Europeans, Quartet, Heat and Dust, The Bostonians* and *Mr and Mrs Bridge. A Room with a View* was released in 1986 to great critical and popular acclaim, garnering eight Academy Award nominations of which it won three. *Howards End* was also nominated for eight Academy Awards, and won three. *The Remains of the Day*, adapted from the novel by Kazuo Ishiguro, was released in 1993 and earned nine Academy Award nominations. *A Soldier's Daughter Never Cries* premiered at the Venice Film Festival in 1998.

In addition to producing, Merchant has directed two television features of his own, a short titled *Mahatma and the Mad Boy* and a full length television feature, *The Courtesans of Bombay*, made for Britain's Channel Four. He directed his first feature film *In Custody*, based on the novel by Anita Desai, in Bhopal, India. The film received several awards including Best Picture and Best Actor in the National Film Awards of India. Prior to *Cotton Mary*, Merchant directed *The Proprietor*. Along with numerous awards, Merchant has been honoured with two honorary doctorates from Illinois Wesleyan University and Bard College.

Merchant has also written several books, including *Hullabaloo in Old Jaipur, The Making of the Deceivers* and *Ismail Merchant's Indian Cuisine*. He is the author of two cookbooks: *Ismail Merchant's Florence* and *Ismail Merchant's Passionate Meals. Once Upon a Time: The Proprietor*, the story behind the film, was published by Bloomsbury. Merchant's latest book is *Filming and Feasting in France*.

Alexandra Viets was born in Dallas, Texas, USA to an American father and a Polish mother. She has lived and travelled extensively in Asia, Africa, Eastern Europe and the Middle East as the daughter of a Foreign Service Officer, spending eight years of her early life in India.

She received her Bachelors degree in Asian Studies from Oberlin College and her Masters degree in film from Columbia University's School of the Arts. After college she worked on exhibition installations featuring Near Eastern art for various museums in the Washington area and for a short period as a freelance journalist at the Centre for Investigative Reporting.

Cotton Mary is her first feature length screenplay, for which she won the 1992-93 New York Foundation for the Arts award. Her other film credits include working as an Assistant Producer on an award-winning documentary, *High Lonesome: The Story of Bluegrass Music*. She has also written *Kashmir*, an original screenplay based on the current political situation in Kashmir, and directed a short film called *Practising English*, on the acquisition of language and culture as experienced by a group of refugees.

She currently works as a freelance journalist, contributing to such publications as the *International Herald Tribune* and the *Asian Wall Street Journal*. She lives in New York with her husband and son.

ISMAIL MERCHANT

Cotton Mary

Screenplay by
Alexandra Viets

PENGUIN BOOKS

Penguin Books India (P) Ltd., 11 Community Centre, Panchsheel Park, New Delhi 110 017, India
Penguin Books Ltd., 27 Wrights Lane, London W8 5TZ, UK
Penguin Putnam Inc., 375 Hudson Street, New York, NY 10014, USA
Penguin Books Australia Ltd., Ringwood, Victoria, Australia
Penguin Books Canada Ltd., 10 Alcorn Avenue, Suite 300, Toronto, Ontario, MAV 3B2, Canada
Penguin Books (NZ) Ltd., Cnr Rosedale and Airborne Roads, Albany, Auckland, New Zealand

First published by Penguin Books India 2000

Typeset in ChelthmITC by SÜRYA, New Delhi
Printed at Rekha Printers Pvt. Ltd., New Delhi

CONTENTS

FOREWORD

Locations have always been a vital element of Merchant Ivory films—though sometimes these locations are not as 'authentic' as they may seem. While the Chateau of Versailles (for *Jefferson in Paris*) was the real thing, the 'room with the view' in the eponymous film was, in fact, a free-standing curtained window-frame, perilously constructed on a platform one hundred feet above the River Arno—which was the only way we could capture a spectacular view of Florence with its cathedral and Gatto Campanile in a single shot.

Our latest film, *Cotton Mary*, involved similar deceptions. Since it was set in Cochin, south India in the 1950s, we needed a colonial house with an established, mature English-style garden. I knew there was no chance of finding such a garden, for the English ladies of the Raj who diligently recreated the herbaceous borders of their homeland in this climactically hostile environment have long gone, and the land has reverted to its indigenous flora of flamboyant bougainvillea, palm trees and ferns. The object, then, was to find a garden site with potential for some radical improvisation. Thakur House, built by the Dutch at the end of the seventeenth century and later enlarged by the British, had a large lush lawn which was an appropriate starting point for the English 'cottage' garden we would attempt to create from scratch.

Herbaceous plants are rare in this tropical environment but we eventually found a nursery four hundred miles away in Bangalore which could supply us—expensively—with delphiniums, lupins, peonies, lily longiflorum, fuchsias, magnolia trees and old English roses, as well as tropical oleander, hibiscus and spathiphyllum. We were also given permission to raid the Mayor's municipal nursery, though we had to pay an insurance fee for the safe return of his cherished plants, and four production assistants were assigned to look after these. At this rate, stocking the garden was eating up too much of our frugal art department budget and still our production designer, Alison Riva, felt the garden lacked the necessary profusion and variety. There was also the problem of continuity: a scene can take several days to shoot, and though it is in the nature of plants to blossom and die, they rarely do so in the course of an onscreen minute, which may take days to produce. Alison decided that in order to fill out what was already there, and for the sake of continuity, we would have to introduce some artificial flowers into the garden. I was very much against this as I felt that artificial flowers would look—well, artificial. But an imaginative production designer can perform miracles, and the paper flowers, dispatched from England, were placed so cunningly amongst the real flowers and the natural vegetation that they were undetectable in the shots, especially the artificial blossoms randomly twined along the climbing roses which trailed around the balcony of the house.

This house presented us with another set of problems. The geography of the layout had to be reversed from back to front to take advantage of certain features such as the view of the sea, and as we were allowed to use only the upper part of the house we had to find other locations for the ground-level interiors, like a kitchen, dining room etc. (But we are old hands at this: Darlington Hall in *The Remains of the Day* was, in fact, a composite of four separate English country houses.) However, all these disadvantages were outweighed by the rose-garlanded balcony and the sweeping views of the Indian Ocean which I knew would look magnificent on film. Above all, the house had its certain 'magic'—it felt right. All four of the films I have directed have involved property as a theme or the focus of the story and I trust my instincts absolutely about whether a place has the right chemistry, so I ignored my colleagues when they urged me to find a less troublesome location.

Furnishing the interiors in the European style of the period was an easier process. Fort Cochin has, over the centuries, been settled by the Portuguese, the Dutch and the English and, as it is quite a remote region with little tourist traffic, it is still possible to find all manner of furniture, artefacts and objects dating back to.the sixteenth century in the antique market of Jew Town in the centre of Fort Cochin. We plundered the market for fat, over-upholstered sofas and armchairs, light fittings and other out-moded British Raj or colonial furnishings.

Some of the more unusual items, such as the large, brass bedstead and cut-glass chandeliers came out of the Bombay bazaars. All the pictures on the walls came from Phillips, the Bombay antique dealer. There were etchings and drawings in the style of Daniel, the English artist who travelled across India, painting and engraving all the monuments and vistas of the country in the late eighteenth century. Alison commissioned an Indian muralist, Shahji Oppukuttan, to paint one of the walls of the study, giving the room an immediate richness and texture. The Chinese motif of the mural was echoed in the oriental fabrics and upholstery which were also found locally in Ernakalum, a busy commercial town across the waterways from Cochin.

So, in a matter of days, we had transformed an Indian tea-planter's house and exotic tropical garden into the colonial house and cottage garden of, co-incidentally, an English tea-planter's family. Anyone visiting Cochin will see the five-hundred-year-old Church of St. Francis, where Vasco de Gama was buried, and the English club exactly as they appear in the film. Thakur House, however, where we shot our domestic scenes, will be harder to recognize.

Ismail Merchant

A NOTE ON ANGLO-INDIANS

Anglo-Indian, a term first used in the eighteenth century by Warren Hastings to describe the British in India and their Indian-born children, is now more commonly used to describe those people of dual British-Indian heritage. Today, living outside the mainstream of Indian society and often described as being caught in a time-warp, the few Anglo-Indians of India are mostly concentrated around the cities of Bangalore, Madras, Bombay, Calcutta, Lucknow and Cochin. They are a small, often impoverished minority, which some have estimated now number as few as 100,000 in a country of close to a billion. Many of the remaining Anglo-Indians in India still cling to their own rituals and customs, living close to one another, often congregated around the local Christian church. Still a central force in their lives, the church is a last remaining connection and identification with the past. Anglo-Indians speak readily of their English past, of the days when life was better, when you could always get a decent cup of tea.

After India's Independence in 1947, a large wave of Anglo-Indian emigration took place. Many wealthier Anglo-Indians went to Australia, New Zealand, Canada and back 'home' to England, seeking acceptance in a Westernized setting. For them, India had become a foreign country where their preoccupation with being British was often met with hostility and rejection. Those Anglo-Indians left in India were a relic of the British colonial past. Whatever alliance they had with the British had become a distortion, a historical handicap that could only be overcome with true assimilation into modern India.

Brought into being by the policies of Portuguese, Dutch and British colonists, the earliest Anglo-Indian community can be traced back to the Portuguese who established a colony on the Malabar Coast in 1498. Later, in the seventeenth century, desiring greater manpower to settle their colony in Madras and a population who could negotiate local customs, the East India Company paid a gold *mohur* for each child born to an Indian mother and a European father.

During this initial period of colonization, the Anglo-Indian community flourished, holding a special status as a distinct English-speaking and Christian community with knowledge of Indian customs, Western values and, most importantly, a fierce loyalty to their British progenitors. With all the conditions set for a natural collaboration, the Anglo-Indians helped generate great wealth for colonial purse-strings. The Anglo-Indians identified with and were accepted by the British, enjoying many of the same priveleges and lifestyle. Under the prevailing philosophy that conditions in India would never suit a British constitution, Anglo-Indians were viewed as providing a needed 'infusion of native blood'.

It was not until the latter part of the eighteenth century that the British began to turn against this community. By then, Anglo-Indians had become so intertwined with their British masters that they looked to England as their place of origin. Concerned with purity of race, and alarmed by how large this hybrid community had grown, the British watched with fear as native uprisings occurred in Haiti and other areas, uprooting colonial rule. Swift measures were taken to restrict the access that the Anglo-Indians had been given. Anglo-Indian children could no longer be educated in England and adults were excluded from obtaining positions with the East India Company.

It was not until the 1857 mutiny that the situation turned in favour of Anglo-Indians again. During the mutiny when the native Indian army vigorously turned against the British, the Anglo-Indians fought loyally against their Indian brethren to save British lives. Deeply shaken by this bloody and violent war, the British never recovered the same level of trust in India. They did, however, want to reward the Anglo-Indians for their loyalty. New positions in the public services were offered and schools based on British principals were established for their children. Jobs were offered in the railways, post and telegraphs, nursing, customs and police, but were given with the caveat that employment was only restricted to the lower grades of the service, with no opportunity for advancement. Anglo-Indians were to be rewarded but still had to be kept in their place.

By the twentieth century, the strange psychological drift of a people alternately accepted and rejected was deeply engrained. Exclusion of Indians from jobs in the professional sphere left an educated and motivated population frustrated and with a low self-esteem. Poverty and unemployment became serious problems for the Anglo-Indian community. Discriminated against and isolated from the rest of India, the Anglo-Indian profile was a painfully lonely one. Struggling to maintain a European standard as a visible means of their identity, Anglo-Indians continued to seek a life that was self-defeating. The issue of skin colour, always of great significance, was ever more important to the Anglo-Indian. A whiter Anglo-Indian could 'pass' as British, whearas a darker-skinned Anglo-Indian might be denied the rightful passage of his dual heritage, the same dubious heritage which he struggled to overcome.

Alexandra Viets

SYNOPSIS

Set in post-colonial India of the 1950s, *Cotton Mary* is the story of two Anglo-Indian (part English and part Indian) sisters, Cotton Mary and Blossom, their niece Rosie, and their tangled and complicated interactions with a British family.

As the BBC correspondent stationed in Kerala, south India on a special assignment, John Macintosh is absent when the screenplay begins with the premature birth of a 'special' child to his wife, Lily, in an old British army hospital. On the night of Vishu, Theresa Macintosh, the seven-year-old daughter is left to find her way through the town and to the local hospital for help. Staffed by Anglo-Indian nurses, including Cotton Mary and Rosie, the hospital sets the stage for the first part of the film. A crisis arises since Lily is unable to breast-feed her child. Despite efforts from the hospital staff, the child is close to death when Cotton Mary comes to the rescue by stealing the child away to her crippled sister Blossom, who is a wet nurse in a nearby Alms house. Still living in the past when her life was peopled by ladies of the Raj and their children—and remembering the time when the Alms house was a vital part of the Anglican church, Blossom and the other Alms house ladies are revived, their status vindicated by having a new 'white' child in their midst. The long hallucinatory night, intercut with scenes of Theresa lost in the dramatic and often frightening Vishu festivities, finally comes to an end when Blossom's milk saves the child. The success that Mary has in arranging for the feeding of the baby makes her indispensable to Lily, who offers her a permanent position in her home as an 'ayah' (or nanny).

Once she is inside the house, Mary's relationship to the baby and her burgeoning friendship with Lily give her a unique position from which to operate. Lily embraces Mary and delegates more and more of her responsibilities to Mary as her own eccentricities and lack of interest in motherhood absent her from the family. Unhappy with the companionship of the very traditional expatriate community and emotionally distanced from her husband, Lily withdraws to her garden and into herself. Gradually, Mary usurps the powers of the loyal family servant, Abraham, whom she accuses of stealing, and more importantly, of being 'dirty'. Ultimately she is able to push Abraham out and replace him as the Master's 'right hand man'. Boasting to the other ayahs that Master is building her a house in England 'near Wellington Castle', Mary begins to achieve the identity she desires.

As Mary continues to insinuate herself, her friend Rosie, beautiful and pale-skinned, also manages to win her way into the British home by concentrating her attentions on John Macintosh. Determined to get the life she wants, Rosie betrays Mary's confidence in her and plays along with the idea that she is helping Master with his 'work'. Drawn to Rosie's beauty and the gradual but determined detachment of his wife, John turns to Rosie as his lover.

Meanwhile, Mary's sister Blossom continues to feed the newborn baby and becomes increasingly frustrated by the lack of attention paid to her efforts. In the final act of rebellion, Mary responds to Blossom's repeated demands that Madam visit her by 'becoming' the Madam herself. She is momentarily triumphant as she strides into the Alms house, her hair newly coiffed, dressed in Madam's clothes, and wearing Madam's shoes.

In the dramatic conclusion, which exposes each of the main characters' often conflicting English and Indian identities, desperation and betrayal lead the sisters, Blossom and Mary, to attack each other's aspirations. The Alms house ladies taunt Mary and reveal the truth about Rosie's relationship with John. As Lily returns to England with the children, John also rejects Rosie.

Mary is left, unable to reconcile her identity, her hopes in ruins and half-mad.

Cotton Mary

ACT I

Hospital

South India. October 1954. A fictitious city on the Malabar Coast. Years of colonization have produced long standing loyalties to the past.

1 EXT. TOWN—NIGHT

The last rays of the afternoon sun settle over a mountain valley. We see the silhouettes of two Anglo-Indian women in nurse's uniforms walking down a hill. One of them is Cotton Mary, small and stocky with blue-black skin and broad south Indian features. Mary's friend, 'Long Hair' Rosie, is beautiful and fair-skinned, almost white. They link arms as the credits roll.

V.O. MARY

I had this kind of dream, ma.

V.O. ROSIE

What was it, child?

V.O. MARY

A baby, ma.

V.O. ROSIE

What baby?

V.O. MARY

It was small, ma.

V.O. ROSIE

What colour was it?

V.O. MARY

White.

V.O. ROSIE

Go on. You're only dreaming, ma.

The sound of their footsteps gradually fades.

2 INT.—MACINTOSH HOUSE—MORNING

A wild and overgrown garden surrounds an old tea planter's house that could pass for a small country estate in Devon.

3

Abraham, fifty, the Bearer, lopes across a darkened room and throws open some dusty shutters letting the morning sun pour into the house. We see him framed in the window, looking out at the view.

3   EXT. MACINTOSH HOUSE—DAY (A FEW WEEKS LATER)

Lily Macintosh, thirty-six, a tall willowy English beauty, is planting in the garden. We see her hands—rough and calloused as she prepares the soil. She places a bush of wild rose in the ground, spreading its long whitish roots, and packs the earth around it.

THERESA (O.S.)

Mummy?

Tired and distracted, Lily doesn't hear. She lifts a hand to push back a loose strand of hair, streaking dirt across her cheek.

THERESA (O.S.)

Mummy, look at the lovely flowers that Mali brought.

Lily looks up to see her daughter, Theresa Macintosh, seven, standing next to her with a stalk of frangipani. It takes Lily a minute to respond. She looks for the Mali.

LILY

Oh, darling. It's beautiful.

Lily holds the flowers and carefully puts them down. Seven months pregnant, she stands up to massage her back. She turns to look at the view, as a pinkish dusk settles across the horizon. Abraham comes across the garden with his dust cloth over his shoulder.

ABRAHAM

Please, Madam. Master is coming for dinner?

LILY
(anxiously)

Why? Did Master call?

ABRAHAM

No, Madam. No phone call. Nothing, Madam. But, it's difficult for Vishu, Madam. Lines are down.

He sees Lily's disappointment.

ABRAHAM

But I'm making Madam's favourite dish. Prawn Masala.

4

Nice fresh prawns today!

Mary and Rosie walk off the path and onto the main road. They enter an old Anglican church. Holding hands, they move to the front of the church and kneel down to pray.

MARY & ROSIE

Our Father, who Art in heaven, hallowed be Thy name. Thy kingdom come, Thy will be done on earth, as it is in heaven.

As we hear the sound of their voices echo through the large cavernous church, the camera travels over Portuguese, Dutch and British names engraved into the walls . . . In the Memory of Our Daughter, Sarah Boyd, 1892 . . . With Loving Fondness, Sir John Lawrence, 1904 . . . F. DeSilva, Ann DeCosta, Father Wiliam Hobart . . .

MARY & ROSIE

Give us this day our daily bread, and forgive us our trespasses, as we forgive those who trespass against us . . .

Mary notices Rosie positioning a small hand mirror so she can look at a young man who has just wandered in. Mary nudges her.

MARY

Eh! Rosie.

Rosie shakes her head but her thoughts are elsewhere. Mary gives her another shove.

MARY
(whispering)

Give some respect child. You come to church and start looking everywhere, every Tom, Dick and Harry. Keep your mind on the job, Rosie.

ROSIE
(annoyed)

What Dick and Harry, it's only the rector's son. And I've something in my eye, ma.

She pulls up the mirror.

MARY
(disbelieving)

Something in your eye, ah? I know what you have in your eye.

She pinches her. Rosie jumps.

MARY

Better listen. Who will look after you like I am! Who found you the job in the hospital?

ROSIE
(obligatory)

Hah.

MARY
(exploding)

What 'hah'! You want to be some kind of village girl, Rosie? Husband will give a nice wallup like that Dorothy DeCosta.

Rosie shrugs, she's heard all this before. She tries to sneak a look towards the back of the church.

MARY

Send your eyes to God, Rosie. Send him your heart.

She smacks the back of Rosie's head as they bow down to pray.

MARY & ROSIE

. . . God bless Mummy, Auntie G. God bless Pinky, Blossom, the sisters, Harriet and Sonny . . . and God bless the Queen.

5   INT. HOUSE—DUSK

Abraham comes through the living room with a tray of evening tea. He stops to turn on some lights and then shuffles slowly across the room, one foot limping slightly behind the other.

ABRAHAM
(to himself)

Coming, Madam. Coming, coming . . .

He stops for a second in front of the mirror, and buttons the top of his jacket before he climbs the stairs. The door to Lily's room is open.

RADIO

Britain and Egypt successfully completed negotiations tonight for a treaty ending their long dispute over control of the Suez Canal Zone.

ABRAHAM

Oh God. Oh Jesus.

RADIO

Dr Mahmoud Fawzi, Egyptian Foreign Minister, announced at the end of the final negotiating session that the Egyptian Cabinet . . .

The radio broadcast becomes static. Abraham's hands shake. He puts down the tray and runs to Lily, lying half across the bed, drenched in sweat. Frightened to touch her, he runs to the telephone on the dresser.

ABRAHAM

Hallo . . .? Hallo?

He shakes his head and calls downstairs for help. Looking up for a second, Lily eases herself against the bed. This last effort drains her face of colour. Her eyes close and her head jerks forward.

ABRAHAM

Oh God.

Abraham looks outside the window, calling loudly, but nobody comes. Theresa's face suddenly peers out from behind the door. Abraham turns and grabs her arm. He holds her firmly.

ABRAHAM

You must run for Mummy. Wires are still down. Doctor must come. Everyone here is gone.

He motions how she must go. Theresa nods, her eyes filling with tears.

ABRAHAM
(frantic)

Master's gone. Car nehe. Run fast for Mummy, go to hospital, Wellington Hospital.

Theresa stands frozen by the door, still staring at her mother.

7

Go! Hurry!

6 EXT. ROAD—DUSK

The sound of a south Indian raga. A single male voice with only a drum as accompaniment. A low melancholic sound which moves in cycles, repeating phrases, and building on the same rhythm.

We see Theresa running furiously through the groves of bushes, down the hill and into the town. Fireworks explode above her, for the festival of Vishu, spraying the streets with coloured light.

7 EXT. HOSPITAL—NIGHT

A thick swarm of moths and bugs encircle a light bulb. Next to the bulb is a sign for the Lady Wellington Hospital.

The sound of car door slamming. The sound of a church bell ringing. In the dark a stream of nurses run out from the domed entrance to the hospital, an old rather shabby hospital built by the British, now run by the Indian army.

The sound of their voices—muffled, foreign. The cadence of their speech high and wavy.

NURSES
(Malayalam)

Hurry, hurry.

Lily is lifted from the back of an old Ambassador car and into a wheelchair. Within seconds she is engulfed by a cloud of white chatter.

8 INT. BIRTHING ROOM—NIGHT (AN HOUR LATER)

Half a dozen nurses in a circle around a bassinet with Lily's baby girl. The nurses whisper. Their pointed caps are bat-like. The light is dim and yellow. Rosie stands across from Mary, watching her.

Mary's hands, small and strong. She pours the oil into her hand and then massages it onto the baby. On its chest, arms, legs.

NURSE 1
(whispering)

What's she doing?

ROSIE

Rubbing with coconut oil.

To oil her limbs?

It's her circulation.

She bends closer.

Can you see?

Ooh, yes!

The baby has a bluish spot on her forehead, that almost looks like a vein at the surface of the skin.

Another nurse takes the baby and places it on a rusty metal scale (the kind you might see at a market). One by one tiny weights are added to the opposite side.

She can't weigh more than three pounds!

Ugly, isn't it. So white . . .

Better to suffocate her and be done with it!

Mary is fully concentrated. A black string with a cross falls across her uniform. The whiteness of her uniform is accentuated by the deep dark colour of her skin.

Rosie overhears the two nurses at the back of the room as they watch Mary.

She's that Anglo-Indian thing?

Hah. She told Matron, this is a child from God. Special child, nah.

Look! She's lighting a candle.

Mary lights a candle in front of a small picture of the goddess Lakshmi, the goddess of wealth and good fortune. The flame sizzles and then shoots up. Some light is cast on the baby's face.

Understanding this to be a good omen, the nurses suck their breath.

9   EXT. HOSPITAL HALLWAY—NIGHT

A worried Abraham sits next to Theresa on a long wooden bench in the hallway. She is fast asleep. Above them on the wall is a painting of Jesus—a dark-skinned Jesus with a garland of marigolds around his neck. The flourescent light flickers, threatening to plunge them into darkness. A night nurse passes by.

ABRAHAM

Madam is alright?

The nurse nods and moves away.

10   INT. LILY'S ROOM—NIGHT

A dozen nurses stand on attention as the Matron leads Doctor Jain, fifty-four, and his male attendant into the room. The nurses in the back are whispering, their sentences overlapping one another.

NURSES (VOICES)
(a jumble of words and whispers)

Edwards family Madam. Child only. Mother passed. England. Hah.

Mary, Rosie and all the nurses stand around Lily's bed. There is a sense of foreboding.

Dr Correa stands at the end of Lily's bed. He is a military man— procedural, abrupt. He speaks with a voice that conveys his authority.

DOCTOR

Good evening, Mrs Macintosh. How are you?

Lily lies on her bed with one breast exposed outside of the sheet as if it were disconnected and separate from the rest of her body.

LILY

I'd like to speak with Dr Martin.

DOCTOR
(surprised)

Madam doesn't know? Doctor Martin is gone. He left

10

India. Some time ago.

Lily hesitates, looking around at the hospital's dilapidated walls, the few traces of English signs replaced by Indian ones. The faces of all the nurses—suddenly so foreign to her.

MATRON
(aside)

Madam's milk is still not coming, doctor. We've given massage, compress and all. Nothing has come as yet.

DOCTOR
(to Matron)

Mrs Macintosh had any fall, some kind of accident?

MATRON

No, sir.

DOCTOR
(to Matron)

First child?

MATRON

Second, sir.

The doctor finishes his examination, still addressing himself to the Matron.

DOCTOR
(lower voice, to Matron)

Madam has some shock. Please give more massage. Her milk must come.

MATRON

Yes, doctor.

DOCTOR

Is your husband here? I wish to speak with him.

Lily flinches, her eyes flooding. The Matron steps forward again, whispering that there has been no word from him.

The doctor exchanges a look with the Matron and then lays his hand across Lily's bed.

11

DOCTOR

I can't tell you lies, Madam. This is a special child, an early child. The body is not fully developed. She's very small and extremely weak.

LILY

I see.

DOCTOR

These kinds of children have all kinds of conditions. The heart is weak. Sometimes the stomach too can be weak. The system may not allow mother's milk to be utilized. We don't know for sure. But the child must eat, Madam. This is her only chance.

Fear and incomprehension fill Lily's eyes. She looks around, searching for anything familiar to latch onto.

DOCTOR

You musn't lose hope, Mrs Macintosh. We'll try every way. Nothing is certain. You must feed the child and you must put faith into your fate.

The doctor motions to the nurses who gather round to comfort Lily. He watches her. The baby cries, lying in a bundle next to her. The Matron stands next to her. Everyone waits. Exhausted, Lily starts to shiver with chills.

MATRON

You're still in a state of shock, Madam. That's normal.

LILY

Another blanket, please. A shawl. I'm feeling very cold.

The Matron rubs Lily's forehead, trying to soothe her. The nurses all gather around, pressing in on her.

MATRON
(crooning)

You're a healthy lady, Madam. Dr Correa told you, nothing bad will happen to you. Everything will be fine, Madam.

The nurses surround her bed and begin to massage her again.

12

Try for Matron, try . . .

LILY

I can't.

MATRON
(frightened)

But Madam, the child must eat!

The Matron takes the baby in her arms. With great effort, Lily tries to sit up. Betrayed by the weakness of her own body, she falls back onto the bed.

MATRON

You heard what Dr Correa told you. This is the only chance.

LILY

Don't you understand? I can't feed her. I don't have anything!

There is a murmur from all of the nurses and suddenly everyone becomes quiet, shaking their heads.

MARY

This is a child from God, Madam.

Matron and the nurses move back as Mary approaches Lily. She is much darker than any of the other nurses, with an oddly shaped stomach.

The nurses whisper among themselves in Malayalam. Their words sound like an incantation. Tears stream down Lily's cheeks.

MARY
(louder)

This is God's child, Madam.

Some of the nurses nod in agreement. Lily looks at Mary.

LILY

What do you mean? What are you talking about?

MARY

Special child, Madam. You are lucky, Madam. God

13

gives this kind of child to show you Madam. What is love, Madam.

Lily pauses, comforted by Mary's strange presence. As the Matron and the nurses begin to leave, Mary stands by Lily's bed, speaking quietly but urgently. She bends down.

MARY

Don't lose your courage, Madam. I'm here, Madam. Don't listen to anybody. These Indian nurses don't know anything.

Lily looks up at her, confused.

MARY

I'm half-English, Madam. Anglo-Indian.

Mary smiles at Lily, trying to reassure her.

MARY

My mother was a nurse, in Ryaputah. Maybe you know this place? She served with only British nurses. And my father was in the British forces. Near Chingalputum. British Captain only, Madam. Here, Madam. Look, I have some photos.

Mary pulls a locket from around her neck. Lily looks at the tiny faded pictures in Mary's hand, barely recognizable, of a small, pale, dark-haired man in army uniform embracing an older darker skinned woman in a nurse's uniform. Lily pauses on the image of the woman.

MARY

My mother, Madam. She was from here only.

Lily nods.

MARY

But I look like my father, Madam. Same eyes and all.

Lily peers into the locket to confirm the resemblance. The photo is too dim to see much of anything. Mary hands Lily some water.

MARY

Now drink it up, Madam. You must wash everything out. Then only you can feed the child.

Lily drinks thirstily. She stares at Mary, the blue-black colour of her skin, the odd bulge of her stomach.

MARY

I always had a big stomach. Born like this, Madam. I'm like this only.

LILY

What's your name?

MARY

I'm Mary, Madam. Cotton Mary.

11   INT. HOSPITAL—NIGHT

The Matron sits behind a large desk at one end of the hallway. She is looking at Abraham and Theresa who are still on the bench. 'Long Hair' Rosie is next to Matron, her hands folded behind her back.

MATRON

The child cannot sit like this all night. Not possible. Tell the man to go home. You must stay with her until Madam is better.

ROSIE
(annoyed)

But Matron, my family is waiting for me. Party, Matron. There are so many others. Staff nurse and all. You can ask someone else?

MATRON

This is an emergency. I'm surprised to hear you talking like this. You do your duties and get ready. Now go and tell him you will be taking over.

Rosie acquiesces.

ROSIE

Yes Matron.

Rosie walks toward Theresa, giving her a forced smile. Annoyed, she turns to Abraham.

ROSIE

As soon as I finish with my rounds I'll be taking the girl.

15

Matron's orders.

There is only a weak bed-light on the table. Lily looks exhausted, huge circles under strained and bloodshot eyes. She mumbles to herself, delirious, unconscious of what she is saying. She watches as Mary cradles the baby, rocking it back and forth. Mary talks to herself, to the baby and to Lily. She looks at Lily now and then, smiling in a firm but reassuring manner.

                    MARY

Of course Mummy will feed you. See the lights, Mummy. Such beautiful Vishu lights.

Lily looks behind her, through the window, at the flicker of lights decorating the night sky.

                    LILY

I can remember tiny yellow lights all over the house and through the garden. My mother wore a silver dress and Ayah put a long white ribbon in my hair. She loved my hair.

                    MARY
                 (excitedly)

Oh yes, Madam! My Auntie told me about the club parties. Even the Queen came one time. And the whole city was glowing.

                    LILY

There was an old porcelain fox holding open the door and all the people passing through, champagne glasses in their hands. Even the trees were glittering because Mali put candles in some of the branches.

My mother took my hand and told Abraham to make me a cup of warm milky tea and he stayed with me watching the fireworks until Ayah took me off to bed.

                    MARY

God gave milk for what? To grow and become big. Eat something, Mummy girl. You are feeling very weak now. You'll be better soon, love.

16

LILY
(frustrated)

Why do you keep saying that? Can't you see, its not working.

MARY
(alarmed)

No, Madam, don't talk like that. It *will* work. What will Master say, he'll be so happy to see his new baby girl.

Mary places the baby next to Lily who stares at her, swaddled in blankets, lying still.

LILY

He'll say its my fault.

MARY

No, no, Madam.

LILY

But I'm very worried. She doesn't look well. The baby doesn't look well.

Mary strokes Lily's forehead, trying to make her relax.

MARY

Baby looks well, Madam. She's very tired, Madam. Madam must rest now.

Mary sits down on a chair next to her and begins to smoothe Lily's hair, gently, steadily, the way a mother would do for a child. She starts to sing.

MARY

Onward Christian soldiers marching as to war, with the cross of Jesus going on before; Christ the royal Master leads against the foe . . .

13   INT. LILY'S ROOM—NIGHT

Lily lies with her arms loosely tucked underneath her head in the darkened room. She is fast asleep. The only light is the orange glow of a small electric heater.

Mary is crouched next to Lily on the floor. She has the baby in her arms

and she is singing. Everything about her seems focused, intense.
Rosie calls into the darkness.

ROSIE

Mary-ma, are you there, ma?

MARY

Ssshhh . . . .!!

ROSIE
(whispering)

Matron ordered me to take Macintosh Madam's child
out. I can't believe it! Mugs and all were waiting for me.
We were going to have a party. It's not fair, ma. Why
so much fuss for these people? If it was Indian child,
Matron won't care like this!

MARY

A child is a child, Rosie. Why do you talk about India
this and India that . . .

ROSIE

Listen to you!

MARY

Child is like me only, Rosie. How I can leave the child
with those hospital people? Madam doesn't trust them.

Rosie broods silently. The two of them sit quietly in the darkness
watching Lily as she sleeps. Mary puts the sign of the cross on the
baby's head.

ROSIE

If the child is not meant to live, there's nothing you can
do.

MARY

God is my witness. Rosie. Nothing will happen to that
child.

She bangs her chest.

MARY

Swear on my mother's life.

ROSIE

But you're not a doctor, ma.

MARY

I will know the way, Rosie. God will always show me the way.

Rosie nods and sighs heavily, preoccupied with her own problems.

ROSIE

You know ma, I think she wants to sack me. She's always after me.

MARY

Yes, yes, Rosie.

Mary gets up and puts the baby into the bassinet. She covers her with a tiny woolen blanket and then covers Lily too. The two women walk together down the hall towards the nurse's station. Mary catches Rosie glancing out the window as if she were looking for someone.

Rosie pulls Mary aside before they go into the ward. She bends towards her with a conspiratorial air and unfolds a piece of paper from her pocket.

ROSIE

But see, ma. Look what Mummy wrote. You must talk to her. She's desperate.

Mary doesn't take any notice. Rosie waves the paper in Mary's face.

ROSIE

Matrimonials!

The top of the page reads, 'Vishu Specials'. The page is a list of personal advertisements.

ROSIE

I'll read it to you.

She throws her head back, shaking out her hair.

ROSIE
(proudly)

One educated lily-white girl looking for one educated bachelor. Fair skin preferred. Balance of East and West values desired.

19

MARY

Lily-white, lily-black. Mama coothele, Mummy. How many colours God sees? Rosie, Rosie. Who's going to catch you? You're going to lose all your self-respect child!

ROSIE
(looking around, embarrassed)

Don't shout, Mary.

MARY
(much louder)

Eh! What do you mean, don't shout. God gave mouth to what? To talk, nuh?

14   EXT. CITY SQUARE—NIGHT

Abraham, Theresa and Rosie walk down the hill towards the city. It is a magical sight. Candles and special lanterns illuminate every house and building. There is no electric light anywhere. Abraham pauses as they near the road, looking worriedly at Theresa. He takes her hand.

THERESA

Don't worry, Abraham. I'll be all right.

ABRAHAM

You go and see Mummy in the morning. I'll be waiting in the house. When you come home, I'll make some nice milky tea. Okay?

THERESA

Goodnight, Abraham. See you tomorrow.

Theresa watches as Abraham moves slowly down the road. Burning to go, Rosie pulls her away.

ROSIE

Come on.

She leads Theresa right through the thick of things, keeping her eyes peeled for her friend, Mugs. She checks her reflection in a shop window.

Wait a minute.

She quickly repowders her face.

ROSIE

One minute! Matron was rushing me so much I didn't
have any time to dress up. I had to go to a party tonight,
but . . . what to do?

*Rosie applies some lipstick and checks her reflection in the mirror. She
leads Theresa to another area where they can see a huge twenty-foot
papier mache statue of the goddess Lakshmi being erected across the
street in the square.*

*Rosie keeps scanning the crowd for Mugs. She's restless. She stands
up, sits down, and stands up again, clearly frustrated.*

ROSIE

I have to go and find a friend. Sit and watch and I'll
come soon.

Theresa looks surprised. She stands up too.

THERESA

Shall I come with you?

ROSIE

No. Better stay here.

THERESA

Will you be back soon?

ROSIE

Five minutes. I'll just be there; near the statue. You can
see me from here, no?

*Theresa looks into the crowd of people, the darkness, the tiny lights
that flicker at the edge. Frightened, she looks back to Rosie.*

ROSIE

Don't worry. Just sit and watch. I won't leave you for
too long.

*She waves and makes her way toward the square. Several children
run in front of Theresa with sparklers. She watches them and when*

she looks around again, Rosie is nowhere in sight.

15   INT. LILY'S ROOM—NIGHT

Three or four nurses stand around Lily's bed. The nurses are once again trying to get the child to feed. They try one side and then the other.

Lily is in extreme pain. She keeps shifting her weight, groaning, complaining, trying to pull away. Exhausted from keeping vigil, the Matron is half-asleep in the corner.

Mary wipes Lily's head with a cool cloth. The baby cries. The nurses eye one another. They speak amongst themselves.

> MARY
> *(worried)*

Nothing. Nothing at all.

> NURSE 1

She can't go on like this, this kind of child will die.

The baby is crying louder.

> NURSE 2
> *(nervous)*

You tried the formula?

> NURSE 1
> *(also nervous)*

Many times already.

Lily's head nods as if she is going to faint. The Matron sees and is roused.

> MATRON

Call Dr Correa!

> MARY

I will look after her, Matron.

> MATRON

What? If something happens, who's going to take the blame?

One nurse rushes out. The other nurse tries to quiet the baby. The first nurse comes back into the room looking worried.

NURSE
(whispering)

Dr Correa has left, Matron. Gone home.

MATRON
(shouting)

What? Left and gone! The doctor must tell me first.
Who's in charge here anymore!

She storms out. The two nurses follow her.

*Lily crosses her arms, shielding her breasts, now rough and swollen.
Mary takes her hand.*

MARY
(whispering)

God will help you, Madam. You will find the way.

She turns away to say a prayer. She holds a small cross in her hands.

MARY
(whispering)

Jesus Christ, our Saviour. We are praising the Lord for
you as a loving gift from above . . .

*Lily looks down at her child struggling to feed and feels sharp deep
pains in her breast as the child pulls away and continues to cry—
terrible hungry cries. Panicking, Lily summons all her strength and
pulls Mary sharply towards her.*

LILY

I can't do any more. Please help me.

*Lily falls back against the pillow, depleted, as if her body had finally
given up. Frightened, Mary wraps the baby and quickly takes her in her
arms.*

MARY

She's with me now, Madam. Don't worry, I'll take care
of her, Madam. I'll feed her.

16   EXT. TOWN—NIGHT

Theresa looks around anxiously. Rosie is nowhere to be seen.

23

Rosie-ee-e . . .!

ROSIE (O.S.)

Theresa! Eh! Theresa . . .

Theresa spins around. Rosie and Mugs, Rosie's boyfriend, dressed in tight-fitting trousers and an open-necked shirt, are running towards her. Rosie shakes her head, as if she were furious.

ROSIE

There you are! Where did you go, I've been looking for you everywhere. What if something happened, who would have taken the blame?

Theresa's eyes flood with exhaustion and relief.

ROSIE

Come on! They're going to be frantic by now.

She looks at Mugs and winks.

ROSIE

You'll walk with us, Mugs?

He agrees. The three of them begin the journey home. Behind them the statue burns until nothing is left but its skeletal underwire.

17   INT. HOSPITAL WARDS—NIGHT

Rosie walks past the same two peasant women sleeping in the hallway. Deep snores emanate from one of the wards. A nurse on duty is half-asleep on her chair.

The door to Lily's room is ajar. Rosie peeps in. Lily is fast asleep. A nurse is sitting in the corner. Mary and the baby are nowhere to be seen.

ROSIE

Have you seen Mary?

The Nurse shrugs.

NURSE

Maybe one hour ago . . .

Rosie nods. She walks down the hall to the other side of the hospital. There's no sound coming from the birthing room. The orange glow

24

from the electric heater warms the room.

ROSIE

Mary? Hallo?

She goes inside.

ROSIE

Mary?

She reaches her hand into the bassinet—it's empty.

18   EXT. FERRY—NIGHT

*Mary sits at the back of the boat holding the crying baby, its face
obscured by bundles of cloth.*

MARY
(to herself)

. . . Hurry, hurry.

*The boat turns into a small mooring. Lights reflected along the edge of
the other side of the canal reveal an extremely poor part of the city.
People living on the streets, some inside huge sewer pipes or crowded
into tiny shacks. Beyond these dwellings are ragged fields. A string of
light bulbs illuminates a long row of tiny shops still busy with the Vishu
crowd.*

19   EXT. ALMS HOUSE—NIGHT

*Made of stone shipped from England more than a century ago, the
Alms house is an almost unreal world, inhabited by the ageing relics
of the British Raj, whose lives remain shaped by the past.*

20   INT. ALMS HOUSE—NIGHT

*A young crippled woman in an antiquated wheelchair peers out from
behind a curtain. She covers her chest with a cloth. Blossom, Mary's
youngest sister, is breastfeeding a newborn Indian baby. She has pale
skin and long wavy brown hair but wears an oversized dress which
makes her look childish, and frail.*

*Her older sister Gwen, fifty-five, a faded beauty, sits next to Blossom.
She has the same brownish hair and pale skin colouring. She sits
chatting with the other Alms house women, all Anglo-Indians.*

*They all wear cotton dresses with neatly tied hair and are an unusual
mix of skin and hair colour; some with very dark skin, blue eyes and
delicate faces, others with very fair skin and wide faces.*

25

Gwen looks contemptuously at a group of poor Indian women in saris—on the other side of the room. Crowded into corners, like the unwanted interlopers that they are, the Hindu women are sleeping, eating, and simply living across the old 'reception room' floor.

GWEN

We'll ask Father Patrick tomorrow when they'll be leaving. It lowers the standard. I found a sack of spices under the bed upstairs! And that's not all. Smelling up the whole place!

Three young Hindu girls celebrating Vishu, brush and dress one another's hair, their clothes vivid oranges and pinks.

An Indian servant woman comes to collect the baby that Blossom is feeding. She hands Blossom a small basket, a present from the family. Blossom lifts the baby off her breast and gives the baby to the servant.

GWEN
(mocking)

Look, they've sent more sweets, sister!

The other women are amused. Blossom smiles generously. Two budgerigars in a cage chatter noisily.

BLOSSOM

No, no. Don't talk like that, child. They've been very good to me.

GWEN

Which family is this, Blossom? I hope they're paying you properly.

BLOSSOM

Khandhur. Ravi Khandhur.

GWEN

Yes, yes. Madam came here once? . . . Tall thing.

Blossom turns abruptly as she sees Mary come in the door.

BLOSSOM

Sister! What a surprise! Praise God.

Mary reaches down to kiss her. Blossom puts the sign of the cross on her forehead. Mary bows slightly to show respect. She uncovers the

26

child. The women gasp.

BLOSSOM

Something happened, sister? Oh God. Give her a chair.

GWEN

What happened, Mary? Whose child is that?

The baby starts to cry. Mary turns all her attention towards Blossom.

MARY
(breathless)

Sister, the child's mother couldn't give milk. A British lady. She came to hospital tonight. I'm worried the child will die, Blossom!

Her voice cracks, overwhelmed with emotion.

MARY

. . . I don't know if it can take mother's milk, sister. Early child.

GWEN

Blossom must try. Give it to Blossom.

Everyone watches as Blossom instinctively reaches her arms out for the baby. Slowly, carefully, Mary hands it to her. Blossom lifts the child to her face, kissing it, caressing it. She seems overwrought with joy. She looks at Mary and Gwen, her eyes filled with tears.

BLOSSOM

It's like the old days! We'll see which baby doesn't take my milk . . .

VOICES OF WOMEN

How long has it been? Sweet, precious. Oh, look . . . Keep it wrapped up!

The old ladies watch, mesmerized as Blossom undoes the top of her gown and draws the tiny white child to her breast, swollen and full—and as the baby finally begins to feed, Blossom looks around, victorious.

BLOSSOM

Sister . . . did Madam send any special instructions? Sister?

21   INT. HOSPITAL—NIGHT (2.00 A.M.)

Mary slips past the sleeping chowkidar (watchman) and into the hospital through a side door with the baby in her arms. She passes a small empty room with the door propped ajar. Theresa is fast asleep on a narrow hospital cot against the wall.

Nearby, two of the nurses still on duty sit around a small table. As soon as they see Mary, there is a lull in their conversation.

One nudges the other who giggles. It's obvious they have been talking about her. The thin nurse turns away and hums and then begins to sing a rhyme in a taunting sort of way.

NURSE 1

You've got a hole in your bucket, Dear Liza. Dear Liza. A hole in your bucket, dear Liza. O' la . . . A hole in your bucket, a hole in your bucket.

Mary hesitates, reaches down to her dress, which is torn at the hem. She holds it self-consciously.

NURSE 2

Mary-ma, your Madam is calling you. Your English Madam was looking for you. She doesn't want anyone but Cotton Mary.

NURSE 1

And Matron was calling for you too. Everyone was looking tor Mary tonight. So important, isn't she?

NURSE 2
(to herself)

A hole in your bucket, dear Liza . . . dear Liza . . .

22   EXT. A HALLWAY IN THE HOSPITAL—DAY

It is early morning. Mary enters the hospital with the baby. She meets Rosie who is still dressed in clothes from the night before. Curious, Rosie stares at her.

ROSIE

Where were you last night, child? I was looking for you.

MARY

Look, look, Rosie. Look inside yourself.

28

ROSIE

What! What's wrong ma?

MARY

Check yourself Rosie, everything will be alright.

ROSIE

Why you're so angry, Mary?

MARY

Go on Rosie! Your mind is somewhere else.

Rosie dismisses her and looks around the room. She sees Mary's bag, her coat, and some tins of food from the Alms house.

ROSIE
(shocked)

You took the baby to Auntie Blossom, ma?

MARY

She's my sister Rosie, why shouldn't I take her?

23   INT. HOSPITAL—DAY

The sun is shining. Lily is sitting up in bed wearing a new hospital gown. Her hair has been brushed, her face washed—but she looks fragile and drained. A nurse is standing by her side, waiting for her to drink her tea. Another nurse opens the door.

NURSE
(dubious)

Your servant is here, Madam.

The door opens and Abraham looks shyly around the door and steps inside, holding a bouquet of flowers from the garden wrapped in a newspaper. Lily's whole face melts into a smile.

LILY

Abraham!

ABRAHAM

Thank you, Madam.

LILY

But where is Theresa?

29

Before he can answer, the Matron peers around the door, her large shadow looming across the floor. Embarrassed, Abraham backs out.

MATRON
(booming voice)

Baby looks so well today, Madam. Good job!

Abraham motions that he will go, waves goodbye and slips out the door.

LILY
(anxiously)

Where is she?

The door closes and then reopens.

MATRON

Oh, here she is!

The Matron leaves as Mary comes in with the baby. Lily's eyes are frozen on her child. She looks up at Mary, anxiously.

MARY

Morning, Madam. Look at Baba. See, she's so fine, Madam.

Mary puts the baby in a bassinet next to Lily.

NURSE

More tea, Madam?

Lily shakes her head, concentrating on the baby. The Nurse smiles, and leaves the room. Lily carefully reaches her hand into the bassinet and puts her finger into the baby's tiny hand.

LILY

What did the doctor say? Is she going to be all right?

MARY

No need to talk, Madam.

Mary holds the baby close to her own body, every bit of her concentrated on protecting the tiny infant. Mary looks down at the baby with fierce attachment.

MARY
(pause)

Please, Madam. Nothing to fear, I can give special care.
Later on, she can take from the bottle. Now she has to
take mother's milk. This kind of children must have. I
will look after her, Madam. You must trust me, Madam.

LILY

But, how did you feed her? What did she eat? I must
know.

MARY

Look here, Madam. We have our ways, Madam. See
how well the child is. You must look and tell me. You
are the child's mother. Only you can say.

*Lily hesitates, looking back and forth at Mary and then at the baby,
swathed in a blanket, sleeping peacefully. She grasps Mary's hand,
reaching out to convey her gratitude.*

LILY

Yes, Mary. She looks well. I'm so grateful to you.

MARY
(interrupting her)

I'm here for the child, Madam. God is with us.

24   EXT. HOSPITAL—DAY (TWO DAYS LATER)

*Rosie sits on the steps of the hospital while the sweeper girl is
sweeping the entranceway with long elegant strokes. Suddenly a large
car makes its way down the long driveway. John gets out, rugged,
unshaven and in need of a shower from days on the road. He
dismisses the driver, steps out and stretches himself. Rosie stares at
him, intrigued. Pleased to see such a pretty nurse, John smiles
flirtatiously.*

JOHN

Hello. What's your name?

*Rosie smiles shyly. Excited, she rushes ahead into the hospital to tell
Mary.*

25   INT. LILY'S ROOM—DAY

Rosie peers into Lily's room and catches Mary's eye, beckoning her to the door.

ROSIE
(whispering)

Quick, quick! Stand up. He's here. Master is here.

Seconds later there is a loud knock at the door. Theresa is lying on her mother's bed. She runs to the door. Mary quickly stands up as John is ushered into the room by the Matron. She stands back, impressed by his handsome looks.

MARY

Madam, Madam! Master is here!

26   EXT. HOSPITAL HALLWAY—DAY

Theresa rushes towards her father who gathers her into his arms.

THERESA

Daddy! I knew it was you! You took so long.

JOHN

How's my little luv? That's my girl. Come on. Give me a kiss.

Lily watches as he rushes forward and throws Theresa up in the air, reaching in his pocket for a packet of bangles, then another and another. She screams with delight as he bends down to put her on his back.

27   INT. LILY'S ROOM—DAY

The nurses watch as Matron takes the baby from Lily and places it in John's arms.

MATRON

Sir, as head nurse in the hospital which was a British military hospital, I must tell you, sir, that we have taken only the top and best care of your family. There is no other place, sir, in all of India, sir, where you would find this kind of care.

32

JOHN

She's a bit small, isn't she?

MATRON

We'll have to fatten her up.

Pleased, the nurses come to congratulate John before they all file out. Mary reaches to take the baby.

MARY

Excuse me, sir, can I take the child now? Madam is still not well. She needs to build her strength, sir.

JOHN

Yes, of course.

Mary takes the baby and urges Theresa towards the door.

MARY

Come on. Let Mummy and Daddy stay alone.

John comes to sit on the edge of Lily's bed. He moves a tray of tea from the bedside table and takes her hand.

LILY

Why didn't you call me?

JOHN

Darling, I couldn't call from the middle of the jungle.

He reaches over to embrace her and pulls her close.

LILY

The baby's not well, John.

JOHN

Of course she's all right. You're just upset that I wasn't here.

LILY

The doctor says she's not fully developed. He says she can't process her food properly.

John pulls away, beginning to realize something is really wrong.

33

JOHN

You can't believe everything the bloody doctor tells
you.

LILY

She's like a little weaver bird that fell from her nest.

*Lily's eyes are brimming with tears. He takes her hand again and tries
to caress it.*

LILY

I wish you'd been at home. I wish you'd stayed. Maybe
this wouldn't have happened.

JOHN

Darling, you just need to rest.

LILY

You're not listening to me, John. The doctor wants to
talk to you. He's coming to the hospital this afternoon.

JOHN

Why does he want to talk to me?

LILY

He wants to help explain things to you. It's very
complicated. I haven't told you most of it.

JOHN

What can I do—I mean you're the one who he should
talk to. I can't do anything about all this.

He paces nervously around the room.

JOHN

Look, if something's really wrong with her, let's take
her back to England. I mean, for chrissakes Lily, I just
walked in the door fifteen minutes ago.

LILY

It's all right. Was it a good trip? Did you get your story?

He stands at the window and sees the car and driver.

JOHN
(calling down)

Laloo! The tape! Take the tape. I have to go and see the driver.

Mary re-enters the room as soon as John leaves. Lily is crying silently.

MARY

Don't worry, Madam. I will look after Baba. I know how to do everything.

LILY

Are you sure? But can you come home with us? Will you be able to stay with us and look after the baby?

MARY

Yes, Madam. Of course I'll come, Madam. Nothing can stop me now.

28   EXT. ALMS HOUSE—DAY

Blossom is sitting on the veranda doing a small piece of needlepoint. Gwen is tidying up. She fixes some loose hair falling out of Blossom's braids.

GWEN

You're always so untidy, Blossom. You must keep yourself up. How will anybody want to hire you?

She calls the servant girl, Mira.

GWEN

Make a place, please. Mary's coming with Baba. She'll need to rest.

The young girl obediently brings another chair.

GWEN

Look, there she is already. Bring some more tea, Mira.

Mary greets some of the people on the steps who stop to admire the baby. Mary greets her sister and waits for Blossom to take the baby. Blossom smiles, keeping her hands folded. There's a long pause. She shakes her head.

MARY

What, Blossom?

BLOSSOM

I can't feed the child, sister.

MARY

Dr Correa said the child must eat or it will die. It's too weak, Blossom.

BLOSSOM

You know I have to wait for Madam to come. That's always the way, sister.

MARY

Wait for Madam?

GWEN

You'll lose the job, Blossom.

BLOSSOM

Oh yes, sister. Madam always comes to see me. All my children are like that. Not one is different.

MARY
(outraged)

Madam can't come, Blossom. Madam is sick! Madam is still lying in the bed!

BLOSSOM
(retreating)

Madam is still sick?

MARY

Uh-ha, what then. Madam asked me to go home to look after the child. She needs help, sister. Hospital is finished. My life is with this child now.

Blossom doesn't react for a minute as she absorbs the impact of Mary's new situation. Gwen looks away, jealously.

BLOSSOM

Home?

Mary nods her head. Blossom looks around herself at the squalor—the crowd, the filth. The other women come to congratulate her. Blossom turns to the women, trying to mask her envy.

BLOSSOM

Oh, Gwen, Mira! Mary's going home with the child. Home to an *English* house!

Gwen tries to look at Mary as if she were happy for her.

BLOSSOM

She'll tell us about the parties, nah? The food and all.

She catches her breath.

BLOSSOM

Oh, sister!

29   INT. LILY'S ROOM—DAY (THE NEXT DAY)

A broom sits on the floor next to a pile of dust. Mary looks around, stripping the bed, collecting Lily's bags into one corner. On the floor next to the bed are a pair of canvas tennis shoes.

Curious, Mary tries them on.

30   INT. ROOMS—DAY

Mary takes the picture of the Queen Mother off the wall and puts it on the top of her clothes in the suitcase. Two of the other trunks are already packed and sitting by the door. Rosie lies seductively across Mary's bed looking at a film magazine. She flicks through the pages and stops at a still from a film showing a couple in an amorous pose.

ROSIE

Macintosh master is good looking, nah?

MARY

Chi! Go on, what a jungly girl you are.

Gwen frowns as Rosie agrees, good-naturedly.

Mary inspects herself in the mirror. A string of jasmine is pinned to the top of her bun. She pulls up her shirt, loosening it around her belly. She is wearing the canvas tennis shoes. Rosie looks interested.

ROSIE

New shoes, child?

Madam gave me. She has exactly same size!

She looks down, admiring them.

FADE OUT.

ACT II

An English House

31 EXT. ROAD—DAY

A mangy-looking horse peers through a curtain of embroidery placed around his head for decoration.

Mary sits next to a large suitcase in the back of the tonga, her arm securing the pile of Lily's belongings from the hospital. She calls out to the tongawallah.

MARY

(pointing)

Front of the house.

Her eyes brighten as the tonga slowly comes to a stop at the gate of her new home.

32 INT. LILY'S ROOM—MACINTOSH HOUSE—DAY

Mary's hand reaches into frame to pick up an empty cup. Her hand pauses next to a photograph of Lily, posing in front of an English country house.

She stops to look at a row of elegant dresses hanging at the back of Lily's closet. Curious, Mary slides them forward one by one, admiring them: Liberty prints, perfectly tailored cuts, pastel colours, soft, smooth fabric. Her hand rests on a golden yellow dress with cornflowers decorating the borders. She pulls it out cautiously, guiltily—and then steps into it, pulling it carefully over her own plain cotton wrap.

As the dress encompasses her body, she smiles and smoothes the silky fabric over her stomach. She turns toward her profile in the mirror.

33 INT. DINING ROOM—DAY

Mary carries the tray down the stairs. She pauses midway to watch Lily from the stairwell. Lily moves around the room (as her mother must have done), attending to the flowers, checking the sugar bowl, straightening a painting.

RADIO

The government of the United Kingdom of Great Britain and Northern Ireland and the government of the Republic of Egypt desiring to establish Anglo-Egyptian relations on a new basis of mutual understanding and firm friendship have agreed as follows . . .

Lily takes a flower and puts it in her hair.

LILY
(to Theresa)

Shall we ask Mary to make a garland for you? A lovely string of jasmine, like all the Indian girls.

Theresa hesitates.

RADIO

Her Majesty's forces shall be completely withdrawn from Egyptian territory in accordance with the schedule set forth in Part A of Annex 1 within a period of twenty months from the date of signature of the present agreement.

Mary walks in with the tray of bed-tea from upstairs.

LILY

Morning, Mary. How is Baba? I was looking for her this morning. You must tell me when you take her out.

MARY
(very reassuring)

Yes, Madam. Child is fine, Madam. Fine. She just now went to sleep.

John walks in with the newspaper.

THERESA

Morning, Daddy.

JOHN

Hello pet.

He opens the paper and lights up a cigarette, motioning for Abraham to serve. Abraham approaches, his old white serving jacket visibly frayed, a middle button missing.

A bit nervous, Abraham pours a cup of tea for John. He reaches too far, pulls the pot back too quickly and a stream of hot tea spills across the table. He starts mopping the table.

Sorry, sir. Sorry. Sorry.

Mary quickly rushes forward with a cloth and helps him, their hands both wiping at the same time.

LILY

John, I met with Dr Correa yesterday. He examined the baby. He said she's still terribly underweight. He said we may have to put her in hospital unless she improves.

MARY

Baby *has* improved, Madam. See how she's eating.

LILY

John, are you listening?

JOHN

Of course I'm listening. But this chap seems to think we've got nothing better do than keep running back and forth to the hospital.

John's voice has a rough edge to it.

LILY

He's doing special tests, John. Of course we have to go to the hospital.

Annoyed, John motions for more tea. Abraham pours again.

JOHN

Better ask Madam for another jacket, eh, Abraham?

Lily stiffens at seeing Abraham so distressed.

LILY

You needn't worry about things like that, John. I'll take care of it. We haven't had time to buy new uniforms.

JOHN

Well, you've got plenty of time now.

Lily notices a small suitcase sitting by the door as John gets up from the table.

LILY

Can't you stay a little longer?

JOHN

Can't. I've got a feature lined up.

LILY

But, John. I've just come from hospital.

JOHN

I had a call last night about an English chap, Gordon, who was killed by his own workers. Tea plantation on the other side of the river.

Lily pauses, a wave of sadness.

LILY

Yes. How dreadful.

JOHN
(to Theresa)

Look after Mummy.

John kisses Lily and then Theresa. He rushes out. Visibly upset, Lily starts to rearrange the flowers in the vase on the table.

LILY

Abraham will show you the larder this morning, Mary. I'm sure you'll be needing some supplies.

Abraham nods, casting a glance in Mary's direction.

ABRAHAM

Yes, Madam.

34 INT. LARDER—DAY

A small window near the ceiling spreads light over hundreds of cans, boxes of food and containers. Mary's hand slowly traces the English and European goods carefully placed on clean papered shelves.

MARY
(reading, slowly)

Dundee . . . Lemon curd . . .

An unopened carton lies on the floor. Mary bends down to open it and pulls out a box of gelatine. Her eyes wander back through the shelves. She reaches deep into the middle of one to look at a box of lavender soaps. She pulls out the lilac-coloured soap and smells one, then slips it into her pocket.

Abraham watches her from behind, and smiles.

ABRAHAM

Everything finished here?

Startled, Mary takes her hand from her pocket and turns defensively.

MARY

Madam needs something more?

Abraham shakes his head and pulls a thick bunch of keys from his pocket. Mary watches him—enviously.

MARY
(surprised)

Madam gives you the keys?

Abraham nods.

ABRAHAM
(authoritative)

I am Madam's right hand man. Anything for Master you must ask me also.

Mary rolls her eyes and claps her hands, then looks at Abraham in a threatening, seductive way. Uneasy, he moves back.

MARY
(pretend joking)

Ohhh . . . Aha, you are Madam's right hand man! Madam's right hand man! We have to wait and see . . . who will be asking who, my man!

35   INT. MACINTOSH HOUSE—NIGHT

Mary and Theresa sit around a small plastic table in the middle of the room. Mary is doing Theresa's hair. They face the mirror. Theresa is in her nightgown.

THERESA

Anyway, how do you know it will grow?

Mary reaches back and with a single motion unknots her own hair. It falls down her back—a thick sheath of black. She shakes her hair dramatically.

Impressed, Theresa cranes her head around.

MARY

Every night you must pull it very tight . . . from the root . . . and make a plait right to the end.

Theresa reaches up to touch her own hair.

THERESA

But I want to cut it like Mummy's hair.

MARY

After, when you get old, then you can cut it. Not now.

Theresa watches Mary in the mirror.

THERESA

You know what I saw by the hospital before we left?

Mary reaches out affectionately to squeeze Theresa's cheek.

MARY

What, sweetie-mummy?

THERESA

A snake! A black one . . .

Mary laughs and smiles knowingly.

MARY

Ah hah. I told you, that's the hair snake. He knew you wanted to cut your hair. He comes to find these girls once every month.

THERESA
(surprised)

Did you see it too?

MARY

Of course!

She starts to laugh again.

44

And if you cut your hair, next time he might try to bite you!

Theresa's hand touches her hair again.

THERESA

Really?

MARY

Oh, yes. Of course. It's true. Why do you think I keep on growing my hair?

Theresa looks at her sister in the crib.

THERESA

Mary . . .

MARY

What mummy?

THERESA

What's wrong with my sister?

MARY

Nothing's wrong, darling. This is God's child, special child.

THERESA

But she's so small . . .

MARY

Madam is lucky. Big baby is too costly. Small baby doesn't take too much food.

THERESA

Mary . . .

MARY

What?

She has finished Theresa's hair which is a coil of braids with one long one sticking out from the rest. It is so tightly braided that it curls up by itself. They both laugh.

A magnificent view. A thick carpet of tea bushes stretching endlessly across the hills. John strides across a field on the outskirts of the plantation to the site where Mr Gordon, an English tea planter, has been recently murdered. A big crowd has gathered. The family dogs (Labrador, Irish setter) bark at the chaos outside the house. Policemen have roped off a group of workers who are protesting angrily at being confined.

John approaches an impressive figure, Inspector Ramji Raj I.P., forty-five, very high class, elegantly dressed in uniform with a lovely long moustache, who is presiding over the inquiry. John reaches out his hand.

JOHN

John Macintosh, BBC Radio, reporting for the Delhi Bureau.

RAJ
(polished English accent)

Inspector Raj. *(Pause)* Delhi Bureau?

JOHN

I understand there's been some trouble here. I don't want to interfere with your work, sir, but I'd like to interview some of these people.

He looks over at the crowd of people, starting to shout.

RAJ

Murder is a big word, Mr Macintosh.

Some of the workers—mostly young men from poor backgrounds, whose fathers and forefathers must have worked on the tea estates—start to shout and gesture to John.

TEA WORKER 1
(Malayalam)

We didn't kill him.

TEA WORKER 2

We don't want any violence.

TEA WORKER 3

They're just looking for any excuse to crack down on us.

JOHN

Inspector, I understand the unions have been trying to make their way onto the plantations—with some success.

Raj fondles his moustache.

RAJ

Yes. Very true.

More shouting from the back.

TEA WORKER 3
(Malayalam)

You British think you can go everywhere and take anything you want.

TEA WORKER 4

The time has come for you to get out.

JOHN

What do the civil authorities have to say, Inspector? And has the District Commissioner had anything to say?

TEA WORKER 2
(Malayalam)

We're only asking for proper wages. What about our children? How can we manage without money?

RAJ

Better talk to the DC yourself. All I can tell you is that these hooligans in front of you were stirred up by an outsider.

Someone from the crowd throws one rock and then another. It nearly hits John. Raj orders his men to advance with their batons. One young man breaks through the barrier and runs toward John.

TEA WORKER 4
(Malayalam)

Take your money and go! Take a warning from your Mr Gordon. We want you *out*.

37   EXT. ALMS HOUSE—DAY

Mary moves the carriage forward. Theresa climbs the front steps to the Alms house and pretends not to see the two women still in their nightgowns who have stopped their card game to stare.

A crowd gathers. Theresa draws closer to Mary as the women's voices rise in excitement at the new visitor.

THERESA

Who lives here, Mary?

A woman in her wheelchair comes out onto the veranda. Theresa stares at her thin crippled legs held in place by metal grips and her long hair plaited like a girl's in two thick braids. Blossom acts as if she knows who she is.

BLOSSOM

Hullo darling! Treesa! Baba's sister . . .

She shakes her hand, welcoming her. Before Theresa has a chance to say anything, Mary quickly takes her down the stairs where some street children are playing.

MARY

Take some fresh air. Stay outside. Go on. I'll call you.

She pushes Theresa along.

THERESA

But I'd like to stay here. Why are you going inside?

Blossom calls out to Theresa.

BLOSSOM

Mummy is feeling better, I hope. Please tell her I send my regards. The baby is so lovely.

Mary nervously pushes Theresa farther down the drive.

MARY

(to Theresa)

Don't listen to her. She's just a crazy. Go on! Hurry up.

She leaves Theresa at one end of the compound.

MARY

(firm)

Go and play . . . Not a word to Mummy or Daddy. One word and you'll have big trouble. Understand?

Reluctantly, Theresa makes her way towards the other children. As soon as Mary is out of sight she circles back and walks up to the door, peering in through a window.

Inside the Alms house and out of sight, Blossom lets the baby suckle, cradling her, bending down to kiss her. Theresa stares, wide-eyed. Impressed, Gwen and some of the women gather around, looking at the baby, Mary's clothes . . .

GWEN

(impressed)

You like it there, Mary?

They examine her shirt, her skirt, her watch . . .

MARY

What a big room I have! Just like the house we had, sister. Blossom and Gwen were too small but I remember. Same style, nah? Wallpaper and all.

WOMAN

Good people, good respect, nah? Not like Indian house . . .

MARY

(bragging)

Oh, no. Not like Indian house. The butler is under me and the sweeper too.

WOMEN

Oh! The butler too . . . Lucky ma that you got that job. English home, nah.

Jealous of all the attention her sister is getting, Blossom wheels her chair closer.

BLOSSOM

Of course, in those days, Madam would always send me something. That was the custom. Now Mrs Jones was a wonderful lady. She came here. She was part of the church group . . . Remember all the parties, sister? *(pause)* And Master . . . he's important, sister?

MARY

Reporter Sahib!

BLOSSOM

Oh, my!

Mary reaches into her pocket and pulls out the packet of lavender soaps from the larder. She hands them to Blossom.

MARY

Madam's regards.

BLOSSOM

Oh! Sister!

She holds the soaps close to her and inhales deeply. Gwen takes the packet to smell for herself.

BLOSSOM

The smell! It's heavenly. Look, sisters! Look what Madam sent!

They reach for the soaps, passing them around. Blossom looks at Mary, a mischievous look forming in her eyes.

BLOSSOM

Tell Madam Blossom orders her to come.

The women cover their mouths, surprised at her words.

GWEN

See how cheeky you are! After all we're doing for you. You should be so grateful!

Blossom covers her mouth, trying to repress a smile which spreads across her face, making her look girlish and pretty.

MARY

Madam will come. But Blossom, you must give more milk for the night. I can't keep on coming like this every few hours. Madam will be angry if you don't give.

38   INT. LILY'S ROOM—DAY

The sound of the baby crying filters in underneath the door as Lily is getting dressed. Lily stares at herself in the mirror, her hands sliding over her chest.

39   INT. KITCHEN—DAY

The morning sun beats down into the empty kitchen. It is spotlessly clean, nothing left on the counters, the cupboards closed. Abraham is putting away the dishes. Mary comes in and looks annoyed to see him there. She carries the baby in a small basket.

MARY

You can go to take a rest now. I'll finish everything.

ABRAHAM

Nothing to do. All finished. There's some rice and curry in the pot.

MARY

No, no, no. I don't eat that food. Too spicy. I don't like it. You can go. I'll call you if Madam needs something.

ABRAHAM

Madam knows where to find me.

MARY

Madam knows but I'm on duty in the afternoon. I'm not like you all. I don't need to take a rest. All you people like to sleep too much.

Abraham nods, not wanting to get into a tussle. As soon as he leaves, Mary looks into the pot and helps herself to a bowl of rice and curry. She uses a fork, awkwardly, and then puts it down, hurriedly thrusting the food into her mouth with her hands—frightened that someone might see her.

Unexpectedly, the door opens.

51

Hello Mary.

Mary chokes down the food and hides her hands, embarrassed to be caught eating this way.

MARY
(quickly making it up)

Just cleaning up. That Abraham man leaves such a dirty mess here. See here—I can't even eat my lunch.

She hurries to clean some small stain on the counter. Lily holds the baby in her arms, close to her chest. Suddenly anxious, Mary reaches out for the baby.

MARY

Child is full, Madam. Madam can try but I don't think Madam's milk can come now. This kind of child won't take more than two times in a morning. Stomach is too small.

LILY

But how are you feeding her, Mary?

MARY

Only mother's milk, Madam. otherwise child won't survive. Doctor can talk but Madam must look at the child. Child only will tell. If you don't trust me, Madam, please let me go.

LILY

Of course I trust you. But . . .

MARY
(interrupting her)

Madam, please. God is looking after this child. Mother's milk is coming for her. She won't get sick. Nothing will happen to this child.

Mary purses her mouth, pausing, diverting the conversation and looking around the kitchen, pointing to some imaginary dirt.

MARY

But, Madam. I don't want any children eating from this

kind of dirt. Sickness will come and then Madam will blame me only. You must tell that Abraham man. Child's health is more important.

LILY

Yes, of course.

40   EXT. GARDEN—DAY (SEVERAL DAYS LATER)

A hot afternoon. Theresa watches from her perch in a tree as the chowkidar opens the gate and salutes. A car drives in. The driver opens the car doors for three of the club women, stopping in for tea. Theresa jumps down out of the tree, startling them.

WOMEN

Hello!

MRS DAVIDS
(to Theresa)

Shouldn't you be in school, dear?

THERESA
(lying)

It's a holiday today.

MRS DAVIDS
(with raised eyebrows)

Is it really? I'll have to ask your mother about that.

Lily comes to greet them at the door, followed by Mary.

OLD MRS SMYTHE

Welcome home! Welcome home, my dear. But under such poor circumstances. I think about your dear mother everyday.

MRS EVANS

We didn't want to come too soon, Lily. One is so very wretched after a baby. But you've managed quite well, all considering.

The women walk through the house, looking around carefully, taking stock of the furniture and all the family things.

Happy to be home, aren't you, dear? Such a shame your father had to sell the plantation. Have you been up to see it?

Lily hesitates.

MRS EVANS

Oh, and look at the garden. Lily! It's almost just as your mother left it, all the things she loved, in the place she loved most of all.

The women fan themselves, watching Lily as she shows them around, pointing to an immense budlea bush around which dozens of butterflies have gathered to feed.

LILY

If we stand around the bush the butterflies will dance in between us. I've seen some very rare ones . . . magnificent colours, large wing spans, unusual for this time of year.

She smiles, and childlike, she reaches out her arms.

LILY

They love to settle on your head!

OLD MRS SMYTHE

Not on mine!

The women stand back, not quite sure what to make of her.

MRS EVANS
(whispering)

Look at her bare feet. I think she's always been this way though. Rather impractical. Lovely looking though.

MRS DAVIDS

Yes.

MRS EVANS

John's from a rather ordinary background. But terribly charming.

On the other side of the garden, Lily continues the tour. She is clearly in her element, in the garden of her youth.

LILY

Over there's where we planted the herb garden. We've
got lots of mint, five or six different kinds. Of course, it's
heavenly with our tea.

She smiles, leading them to a lovely table laid for tea.

*Mary serves the women their tea and then stands by Lily's side. Mrs
Davids pours herself more tea, glancing first at Mary then at Lily,
clearly ill at ease with the ayah's unorthodox behaviour. She motions
for Lily to tell her off, then hands Mary some flowers she has brought.*

MRS DAVIDS

Can you take these inside for Madam . . .

*As soon as Mary takes the bouquet into the house, the women relax
and sip their tea, studiously watching Lily as they eat their cakes.
Anxious to join in the conversation upon her return, Mary takes a chair
next to Lily. The women stiffen again.*

OLD MRS SMYTHE

Lily, why don't you ask your ayah to bring the baby?
We're all desperate to see her.

*Lily nods to Mary to bring the baby. The women look askance as Mary
rises reluctantly from her chair.*

MRS EVANS

You really have to be much tougher with the servants
or you'll end up in terrible trouble.

LILY

Don't worry, Margaret, I've had plenty of experience.

MRS DAVIDS

Darling, you were just a little girl. You've no idea how
they've changed. Look at that Gordon business. Man
was murdered in cold blood by his own staff.

*The mention of Mr Gordon sends a chill through the conversation until
Mrs Davids lets out a shrill cry as Mary approaches with the baby.*

MRS EVANS

Oh, she's tiny! Bring her here . . . look how fragile she

is, darling . . .

The women crowd around Lily, peering down at the baby. Mary responds with pride as Lily holds the baby.

MARY

Careful, Madam. Head must stay up, otherwise breathing is difficult.

Mary leans against Lily's chair again, watching the baby like a hawk.

MRS EVANS
(worriedly)

You're going home for more tests, aren't you? I wouldn't trust these people. Not with something like this.

LILY

John thinks the doctor's a bit too pushy, but I rather like him.

The women eye each other.

OLD MRS SYMTHE

You must listen to John, Lily. I'm sure he's right.

MARY

Too many tests are not good, Madam. This kind of children needs love only, Madam.

Mrs Davids nods politely.

MARY

She's like my own child, Madam. No difference.

The women look at Lily, taken aback by Mary's continued presence in the conversation.

LILY
(explaining)

Mary looked after the baby in the hospital.

MARY
(protesting)

No, why, Madam! That's the truth. She is like my own child.

The women smile uncomfortably at Mary's insistence.

56

OLD MRS SMYTHE

Where's your ayah from, Lily?

LILY

She's . . .

Mary interrupts her.

MARY

I'm from Thousand Lights, Madam. My father was a British officer with the regiment. You can ask Madam.

She looks at Mrs Smythe, the eldest and most traditional-looking of the group.

MARY

I'm like you only.

OLD MRS SMYTHE

Oh dear!

Mrs Davids looks at Lily, her eyebrows raised. The other women turn their faces away, unsure of Mary's meaning. Lily sees that old Mrs Smythe has gone pale. She pours more tea.

LILY

Thank you, Mary. That's all for now.

The women shrink back as Mary finally exits. Mrs Evans looks at Lily sympathetically.

MRS EVANS

You must know they're particularly difficult, Lily. Your mother must have told you that Anglo-Indians have the worst characteristics of the Indians and the worst of the British.

All eyes are on Mrs Evans as she clears her throat and stands up as she begins to recite, her eyes sparkling.

MRS EVANS

He cannot be a soldier.
There's no room as a clerk.
He is not wanted by the merchants.
His skin is rather dark.

His rise was our own father who gained for us the land.
But to be one with the darky son we will not understand.
Nor can he with the Hindu stand equally on swearing.
But eats his fill and like John Bull has English ways and
      airing.
Why don't the good-for-nothings pack up and emigrate
And leave the run to Babudom and go to Utah state.

Shouts of 'Bravo!'

41   INT. ROSIE'S HOUSE—DAY

Rosie and Gwen sit on the bed in the sitting room watching Mary as she changes the baby. It's a small place, decorated with some pretension: lacy curtains, a large china bowl, a bottle of perfume still in its box.

Gwen is playing a game of solitaire, her nails a vivid shade of red.

THERESA

Rosie, will you make a plait with my hair?

Rosie nods, distracted by Mary.

GWEN

Go on. Rosie. Make a plait for Treesa. She's such a nice
girl. You must make friends with her. Maybe she'll take
you to her house.

Finished with the baby, Mary straightens herself up, combing out her hair.

GWEN

My, Mary's looking so smart. Look at her, Rosie! She's
changing, no?

She takes a closer look at Mary's top.

GWEN

What a beautiful patten . . . English cotton, nah?

ROSIE
(teasing)

Cotton Mary only likes English cotton. Not Indian cotton,
uh?

You bought it?

Theresa looks at Mary's shirt.

THERESA

That's Mummy's shirt.

MARY
(annoyed)

Madam just throws everything. She has too many clothes.

ROSIE

Tell us . . . Madam has parties?

MARY

Oh yes. All the time.

ROSIE

I heard from Susie Auntie that Master likes big dinner parties. She said he came to her house—talks very well!

MARY

Oh, Master talks very well.

GWEN

Rosie told me Master is reporter. BBC and all!

MARY

Hah jee, he travels all over.

GWEN

If Master gets transferred they'll take you too?

MARY

Of course! Who's going to look after the child!

GWEN

See, Rosie . . . You have to take a job like this. You can go home to England and leave this place.

ROSIE

Stop it, ma . . .

GWEN

I told Rosie she should leave the hospital. She has to find a better job. Why to stay? But she doesn't listen to mother. Mother gives her a headache!

ROSIE

It's a good place, Mary?

MARY

Why don't you come over, nah?

THERESA

If she comes I can show her my bangles.

MARY

Come.

GWEN

She'll be lucky!

MARY

She can start with something. Then after, maybe some kind of ayah work.

Rosie stands up, her eyes suddenly smarting.

ROSIE
(protesting)

But I don't want ayah job.

GWEN

Why not!

MARY
(sympathetic)

You have to take what comes, nah. You can change it later.

GWEN

Whole world is changing and this child is sitting still.

Three of the club ladies are bustling around, getting ready for a run through of Charlie's Aunt, *the season's play. The stage is being set by various bearers who walk around holding pieces of furniture until they are instructed where to place them. A few ayahs with children stand around. Mary stands with Theresa and the baby's carriage, watching with great interest. The club manager, Mr Panamal, very self-important, with a chequered neck scarf, trails behind Mrs Davids.*

MRS DAVIDS
(to Mr Panamal)

Move the children away, please. *(To her friend)* Gladys, have you rounded everyone up?

Two of the 'actors' are walking around, rehearsing some of their lines.

MRS EVANS

I can't find Tony anywhere. And I just got a message that Alfred is sick.

MRS DAVIDS

Oh, dear. Well, let's try and get John.

MR PANAMAL
(to ayahs)

Madam wants all the children out of the way. We're going to start. Please take a place in the garden. There's no room here.

He looks directly at Mary who glares back at him, offended by his manner.

MR PANAMAL

Take a step back, please. Madam needs to clear the space.

The ayahs eye him up and down. He adjusts his neck scarf and motions them away.

MARY

Children must watch. We also like to watch. Club is for everyone. We're not troubling you.

MR PANAMAL

Everyone out.

AYAH 1

Be careful, ma. Club manager. Very important, uh. See how he dresses. Neck scarf and all.

MARY

I know this type of fellow. One-side-here one-side-there fellow. *(Loudly)* My father was reading Shakespeare. We know all the stories. He doesn't even understand what is the play about.

43 EXT. BADMINTON COURT—DAY

John has just finished playing a rigorous game. He is sweating—wiping himself down as a group of ladies surround him, trying to recruit him for the play. He resists flirtatiously, enjoying the attention.

MRS DAVIDS

You must. You'd be perfect. It's such good fun. You can't be in India without doing at least one play.

JOHN

I'm no good. Honestly. Not in your league, ladies. I'm sure you have others. Not to mention the fact that I'm hardly ever here.

MRS EVANS

Just do it for fun. We'll worry about the rest later. You'll be marvellous. Won't he? Go on. We can't do without you.

Lily wanders onto the court holding some books from the library. She is lovely looking but wears a wraparound skirt (or the equivalent for the '50s). The women smile politely, if a touch condescendingly.

MRS DAVIDS

Hello, dear. Are you well? You look so much like your mother. Doesn't she, Gladys? We're desperately trying to convince your husband to do a run through of *Charlie's Aunt* with us.

MRS EVANS

But what about Lily? She'd make a wonderful Kitty! We have a lovely costume for you.

MRS DAVIDS
(less enthusiastic)

Yes, of course. Lily must be in it. She looks perfectly well suited for Kitty or even Amy. Go on, Lily.

Lily backs away, trying to withdraw.

LILY

No, no. I can't. It's almost lunchtime, I just came to find the children.

MRS EVANS

We'll all be together. You need a good distraction. We'll even do a dress up, just for fun. Absolutely. I won't hear another word.

LILY
(vigorously)

No. I just can't. I must go.

Startled, the ladies turn to John, urging him on. Embarrassed by Lily's response, he jumps up decisively.

JOHN

I haven't done this since I was in school, but I wasn't all bad then.

INT/EXT. CLUBHOUSE—DAY (LATER)

Focus on the ayahs' and bearers' expression as stage lights go on and John emerges from the changing room dressed as (Charlie's Aunt) Lord Fancourt, in women's clothing, with wig. The club ladies clap and titter, the men egg him on. The bearers seem to witness all this with subdued reaction.

MRS DAVIDS
(whispering/teasing)

Isn't he gorgeous? Look at his legs!

KITTY

I hope your journey from town hasn't tired you.

LORD FANCOURT

Oh no! It was very jolly. Pleasant, I mean. *(Aside to Jack, holding up flowers)* What the deuce am I to do with these things?

JACK

Stick 'em in your dress.

John puts flowers in dress, tries to see over them, can't, so parts them and peers between them. Everyone on the stage starts to laugh as John struggles. Mary watches seriously—without laughing—only nodding her head, as if to commend John's excellent performance.

AMY
(to Charlie)

You look worried, Mr Wykeham. Are you ill?

CHARLIE

No. I'm anxious, I'm—

JACK
(coming to the resuce)

He's a little affected at meeting his aunt today for the first time. *(Aside to Lord Fancourt, prodding him)* Why the dickens don't you say something?

LORD FANCOURT

What the dickens am I to say?

JACK

Talk about the weather.

LORD FANCOURT

Charming weather.

KITTY/AMY
(together)

Oh, yes, delightful. Oh yes, it is charming.

Mary stands directly in front of a side entrance to the stage, her posture defensive and unyielding.

Not nice to make Master dress like that. Let him take another part, that'll be much better. So many other parts. He can take one. I'll tell Madam.

In the middle of everything, Mrs Evans bumps against Mary on the stage. She gestures angrily to Mr Panamal. Fed up, Mr Panamal comes toward Mary and motions her away with the quick, dismissive gesture used for beggars.

MR PANAMAL
(low voice, Malayalam)

This is not your place. Go with the ayahs. I won't tell you again.

The ayahs shake their heads as they watch Mary from the garden.

THE AYAHS

Mary's Master . . . Cotton Mary's Master . . . Look at her, see what she's doing.

MARY
(loud voice, offended)

I can't speak English? I'm working with an English family and I can't speak English?

Mary glares at Panamal, her eyes burning. She turns to the ayahs, speaking loudly, gesturing to Panamal.

MARY
(bitter, to herself)

That black bugger wants to be a burra sahib. Big man! 'Gentleman in the rank, nothing in the bank.' He just dresses like that. Go home, you'll see a small hut.

The ayahs titter and giggle, covering their mouths with the end of their saris.

MRS DAVIDS

Mr Panamal, what in the world is going on?

Brushing off the noise as a servants' quarrel, the actors continue with the play, rehearsing from another scene. John really hams it up, beginning to enjoy himself.

LORD FANCOURT
(smoking a cigar)

By George, here's a find! *(Looking towards door)* I
wonder how long he'll be! Hanged if I don't chance it!
*(Lights cigar with match which he strikes on his boot.
Comes downstage, puffs vigorously)* Beautiful! Beautiful!

Enter Donna Lucia with Ela.

DONNA LUCIA
(sees Lord Fancourt smoking)

(Aside) She's smoking! Ahem!

*He is startled, draws in a large mouthful of smoke, then hides cigar,
holding lighted end reversed in palm—mouth full of smoke—looks
from Donna Lucia to Ela and then straight ahead in agony, holding
smoke first in opposite cheek to each one he looks at, then in both
cheeks, screwing up eyes, almost bursting.*

*At the back of the room, standing next to several bearers, Lily watches
John. We hear the words of the play and see John from Lily's point of
view—his face surrounded by a wig, the nods and winks he exchanges
with the other actors, the exaggerated gestures with his hands. There
is a kind of detached sadness about her observation of him.*

DONNA LUCIA
(aside, behind her fan)

I never knew such effrontery. *(Returning)* Do you know,
Donna Lucia, I'm surprised you don't indulge in the
habit of smoking—so many Brazilian women do, you
know.

LORD FANCOURT

Well, to tell you the truth, that's just what I was doing
when you came in. *(Shows cigar in left hand)*

*Everyone bursts out laughing and comes to congratulate John. A break
is called and John moves sidestage where he starts to flirt heavily with
one of the actresses.*

*Lily smiles blandly and moves away. She walks far across the club's
cool and pristine lawn and finally stops in front of the Mali who is
squatting over a bed of flowers. She watches the quick, rhythmical
way his fingers pluck out the tiny weeds. She bends down on her*

Cotton Mary (Madhur Jaffrey) and Mattie (Nadira) watch to see if Blossom can feed the baby.

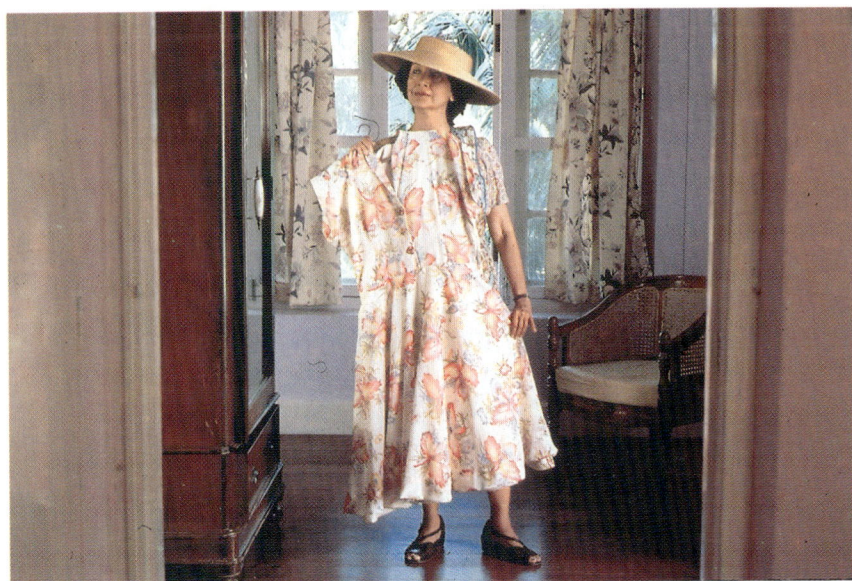

Cotton Mary tries Lily's dress on.

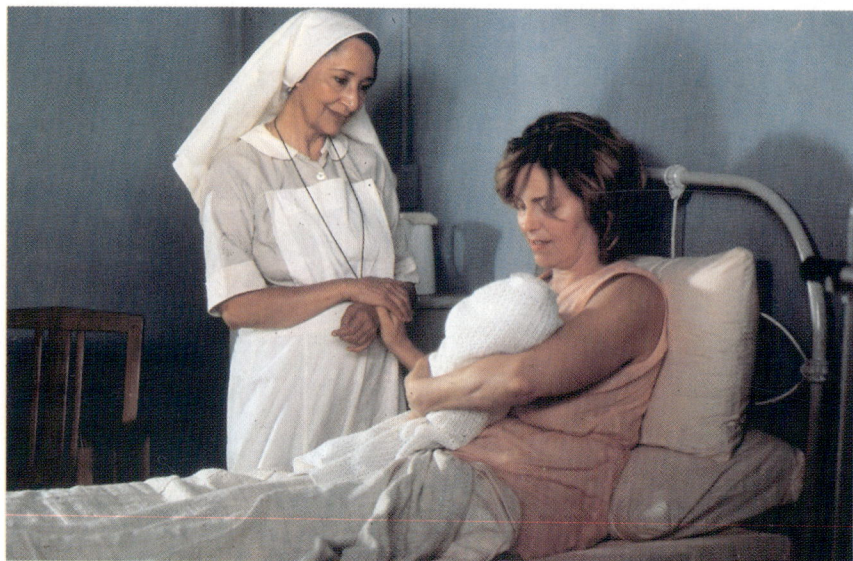

Cotton Mary with Lily (Greta Scacchi) and the new baby in the hospital.

Theresa at Dartington School for Girls. A science class in the 3rd standard.

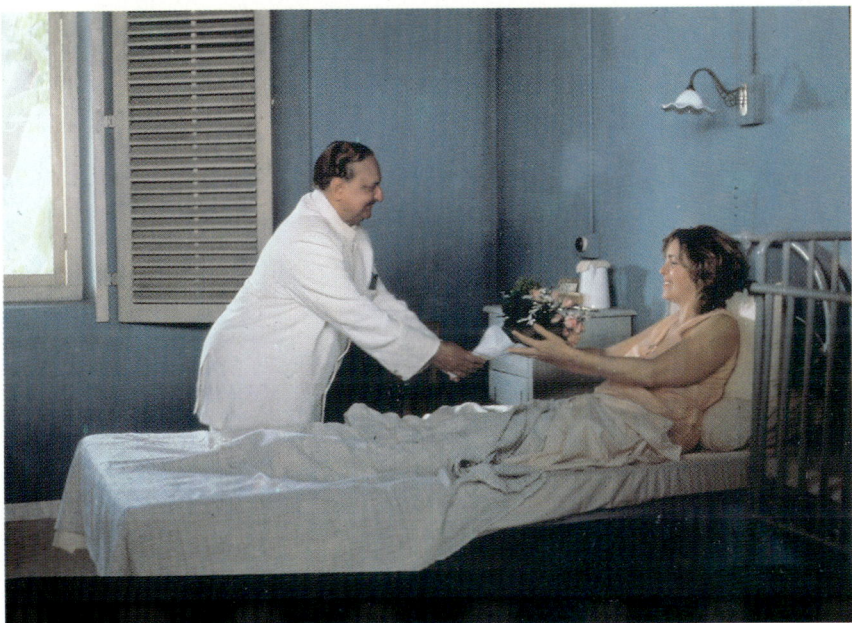

Abraham (Prayag Raj) brings Lily flowers after 'Baba's' birth.

Blossom (Neena Gupta) confronts Cotton Mary at the Alms house.

Lily in the garden of the Macintosh house.

The Alms house. Waiting for 'Madam's' arrival.

Cotton Mary tries to convince Lily that Abraham is stealing from the larder.

Cotton Mary shows Rosie (Sakina Jaffrey) the house as Abraham watches.

Gwen (Surekha Sikri) playing cards at the Alms house.

The three sisters: Gwen, Mary and Blossom.

The English ladies and Lily admiring the garden.

Cotton Mary admonishes Rosie at the hospital.

Lily and John (James Wilby) in the garden of the Macintosh house.

Director Ismail Merchant with writer Alexandra Viets.

knees next to him, picks up some soil and lets it run through her fingers.

LILY

Hello.

The Mali nods. Lily points to the tiny flowers and seedlings that the Mali is transplanting.

LILY

Those are so lovely. They look like a kind of violets we used to have down the path along the hillside. My mother planted them with our Mali.

She holds out her hands, still dirty and worn from work.

LILY

I am a gardener too. *(Malayalam)* I am a gardener too.

The Mali seems oddly pleased. Lily sits on the grass next to him, and reaches out to give Mali his spade and then picks out a weed in the flower bed nearest to her.

On the club veranda, John follows the actress outside to share a cigarette. They look out over the club's grounds. The actress sees Lily on the ground next to the Mali. She points and nudges John, and covers her mouth, laughing. John pulls the actress inside.

JOHN

Come on.

44   EXT. SERVANTS QUARTERS—DAY (THE NEXT DAY)

A small courtyard behind the house. Mary sits on a charpoy (string bed) with a large pan of rice picking out the impurities. Her movements have a peaceful, meditative quality.

There's a knock at the back door and Rosie looks around the corner. Mary quickly puts down the pan but Rosie sees.

ROSIE
(laughing)

Rice duty! You're becoming a kitchen ayah! I thought you were a high class Madam!

MARY

Rosie!

Rosie looks around at the house, duly impressed. She's beautifully dressed in a silk sari. She hands Mary a box of Cadbury's chocolates.

ROSIE

From Mummy.

Mary wipes her hands.

ROSIE

Madam and Master are here? You said something?

MARY

Don't worry! Madam's in the garden, nah. I'll show you the house, then we'll talk with her. She'll love to see you.

Their voices fade as they go into the kitchen and through the house.

45 INT. LIVING ROOM—DAY

Abraham is dusting as Mary pulls open the curtain. He recognizes Rosie from the hospital and watches carefully as the two of them make their way through the house.

ABRAHAM

Madam knows you brought someone?

Mary hardly acknowledges him. Rosie recognizes him from the hospital.

MARY
(whispering)

Madam's 'right hand man'.

Rosie eyes him disparagingly and falls back on the couch and strikes a pose—her arms spread across the back, her legs crossed.

ROSIE

Tea, please!

ABRAHAM
(to Mary)

Shall I call Madam?

Surprised, Rosie quickly gets up.

MARY
(laughing)

No no. Come on Rosie. Get up. I'll tell Madam myself.

Uneasy, Abraham watches as Mary chases Rosie up the stairs.

46   EXT. STAIRWELL—DAY

Mary leads Rosie through the rooms, continuing to point various things out about the house as they go along. She opens the door of the linen closet and ceremoniously runs her hand along the neat piles of white cotton sheets.

MARY

All English made.

Mary closes the door, leads Rosie down the hall and carefully opens the door to Lily's room, which is empty. She streches out her arm with great pride.

MARY

The master bedrooms.

She walks silently around the room, inspecting everything, blowing away the dust, making sure everything is just so. Rosie picks up a bottle of perfume and starts to smell it. She puts it back and sits on the bed. She bounces on it, once, then again.

ROSIE

Mmmmm . . . Too soft, ma!

JOHN (O.S.)
(shouting)

Lily! Lily! There's no towel in here.

MARY
(whispering)

Eh! Rosie! Get up from there! Quickly!

Terrified, Rosie jumps up and stands behind Mary. They step back into the hallway. The sound of a door slamming. John emerges, and grins, seeing Rosie.

JOHN
(surprised)

Hello! Do I know you?

Mary and Rosie press themselves against the wall to let him pass. Rosie nods politely.

MARY

Sir, you remember Rosie, sir. From the hospital?

John smiles, his eyes wandering over her face.

MARY

I'll ask Madam, sir, but if you know of any jobs, sir.

We watch from John's POV . . . Rosie's hands nervously fixing her dress, her hands reaching over her neck, against her waist, the colour of her skin, her bangles sliding. She inadvertently catches John watching her. Their eyes meet. Rosie's gaze is bright and spirited. She smiles and pushes herself forward.

ROSIE

Hello, sir. Nice to meet you. Mary Auntie is helping me to look for a job, sir.

MARY

You see, we're from the same place, sir. She's my sister's child.

JOHN

And what kind of job are you looking for, Rosie?

ROSIE

Something useful, sir. I'm a bright girl, sir.

John pauses, assessing her. He reaches to shake her hand.

JOHN

Yes, I can see you are.

He walks past them down the stairs, waiting for a few moments. When he turns back, Mary has disappeared from view but Rosie is still there.

JOHN

How about a translating job, nothing too complicated? I'd pay by the hour, anything you'd be interested in.

Rosie smiles back, meeting his gaze.

ROSIE

Oh yes, sir.

47 INT. THERESA'S ROOM—DAY

Abraham bends over Theresa's bed, laboriously tucking in all four corners of the bedcovers. From the next room we can hear the sound of the baby crying. It continues. Abraham hurriedly finishes up and goes into the hallway. He looks around.

ABRAHAM
(calling)

Mary?

The baby keeps crying. Abraham pauses, then knocks on the door before he opens it.

ABRAHAM

Mary?

The room is empty except for the baby. He approaches her nervously, shaking his head, protecting his ears from the crying.

ABRAHAM

Okay, okay, Baba. Ssshhh . . . Good girl.

He makes a face, then some strange and funny sounds, hoping to calm her. He picks her up and cradles her until finally her crying dissolves into tired sighs and he notices the warm wet feeling against his arm.

48 EXT. GARDEN—DAY

On his way to the club, John stops in the garden, looking for Lily. Annoyed, he sees her weeding the garden, wearing her Indian wraparound skirt, and a large sun hat. He tries to make some contact. Preoccupied, she ignores him.

JOHN

Come on, Lily. Come and join in with the play. We need everyone we can get.

LILY

Really? From what I could see, there was plenty of interest the other day.

He pauses, looking at the garden.

JOHN
(short)

Happy gardening.

He leaves, disgusted. Several moments later, Mary and Rosie walk into the garden, passing John as he walks to the house. They are both giggling and laughing.

MARY

I brought my friend to see you, Madam. She's from Thousand Lights, Madam. I told her you might know of some possibility for job, Madam.

Rosie comes closer, as if she were going to shake Lily's hand. Lily looks past her at Mary.

LILY

Not now, Mary, I'm busy.

Mary and Rosie exchange looks.

MARY
(taken aback)

She's my sister's child, Madam. It's my responsibility, Madam.

LILY

That's all, Mary. I told you. I'm busy.

Rosie gives Mary a nudge. She motions that they should leave. Just then Abraham comes into the garden holding the baby. He seems embarrassed in front of the three women and tries to explain.

ABRAHAM

Excuse me, Madam, I think the child has to change, Madam.

Lily suddenly whips around to face Mary.

LILY

Can't you do that yourself, Mary? That's really not Abraham's job.

She turns away, her face red from anger. Stung, Mary grabs the baby from Abraham and walks away. Out of earshot, Rosie shrugs, trying to console her friend.

                           ROSIE

Never mind, ma. They're always like that, nah? English
Madam . . .?

49   INT. HOSPITAL—PEDIATRICS—DAY

Lily walks quickly past a sick man lying in the hallway outside the doctor's office. A group of Indian mothers clutch their babies, some of the children are crying. Lily stares at a woman nursing her child. A small thin nurse finally opens the door to the office.

                           NURSE

Mrs Macintosh? Doctor Jain will see you now.

Doctor Jain sits behind a large neat desk. He gestures for her to take a seat.

                           LILY

Thank you for seeing me, Doctor Jain.

                          DOCTOR

Yes, yes. How is the baby? You didn't bring her today?
And how are you feeling?

                           LILY

All right, thank you, but I'm afraid I'm still having
problems with the feeding. She can't seem to get
enough milk. I've been wondering if I might be ill.

                          DOCTOR

But Mrs Macintosh, I have given you a very thorough
physical exam. You are quite healthy. I can't find
anything wrong with you.

He sees her concern.

                          DOCTOR

But you may be still too weak. You must take rest. A
trip to the hills would do you some good. A different
view. You've had quite a lot of changes recently.

73

LILY

Yes. That would be nice. Doctor Jain, were you at the hospital when Dr Martin was working here? He was our family physician when I was a girl. And he looked after my mother. She wrote about him in her letters.

DOCTOR

I'm sorry. That was very long ago. I was not here at that time. You might ask some of the nurses.

LILY

Is there something else I should do, doctor?

The doctor studies her carefully.

DOCTOR

Yes, yes, Mrs Macintosh. You must start a special diet and some exercises too. I will write it for you. Little by little I believe you will improve.

50 INT. KITCHEN—NIGHT (THE NEXT NIGHT)

Mary is preparing some tea, with one arm holding the baby on her hip. Both Abraham and Theresa are also in the kitchen. Mary has a large scarf wound around her head, like a huge bandage. She mutters to herself as she pours sugar into her cup.

MARY

I can't work like this. Madam doesn't show me respect. Who's going to give . . . we slave for these people, and what? Why to stay? If not for that child why shall I stay . . . I'm going to go, Baba . . .

Abraham shakes his head at her, motioning to Theresa, trying to tone her down. Lily comes into the kitchen. Mary walks past Lily—bristling.

LILY

Mmm . . . What's Mary making for dinner?

MARY
(under her breath)

Mary making . . . Mary is making.

Lily looks at the scarf tightly wrapped around Mary's head.

What's wrong, Mary?

MARY

Nothing's wrong, Madam. Too much talking.

Mary brushes a tear from her face.

MARY

I can't work like this, Madam. I better go. You can find someone else to feed your baby.

Lily looks at her, nervously.

LILY

What are you talking about? What's the matter?

MARY

Nothing, Madam. Nothing. Let that man look after the baby.

Worried and upset, Abraham turns away, trying to continue his cooking.

LILY

What are you saying about the baby?

MARY

You talk to me like that outside, why Madam? We're just poor people, not nice to talk like that.

LILY

Oh, for God's sake. I didn't mean anything towards you. I couldn't manage without you. You know that.

She hesitates.

LILY
(imploring)

You can't go, what would I do without you?

She reaches for Mary's hand. Mary moves away from it. Instead she thrusts her hand toward Abraham, who finally leaves the room— disturbed and embarrassed.

MARY

Go, go, Madam. Leave me. That man will look after

you. He's your family servant. I'm just from the road.
Let him look after you, Madam.

51 EXT. MACINTOSH HOUSE—DAY

*Rosie opens the wooden door at the back entrance to the house and
walks carefully into the courtyard. She watches as the dhobi's hand
moves expertly over Lily's pink skirt. His fingers sprinkle the right
amount of water . . . the thick iron blade slides across the fabric into
a quick burst of steam.*

MARY (O.S.)

Rosie!

Startled, Rosie spins around.

ROSIE

Afternoon ma. I brought important papers for Master.

She hesitates, trying to find the right tone.

ROSIE
(eager)

You know he hired me, ma!

MARY
(disbelief)

Master hired you?

ROSIE

Yes, ma. For translating work.

MARY
(doubtful)

What kind of translating work?

ROSIE

He's making an article, ma. Health system.

Mary looks at her friend for a long time.

MARY

What health system! Rich people health or poor people
health?

Rosie shrugs.

                    ROSIE

I have to travel with Master. We have to take private
boat and all.

                    MARY

What? He told you that?

                    ROSIE

Oh yes. He said, he said he wants full cooperation.

                    MARY

Madam won't let you travel like this. She doesn't like it.

                    ROSIE
                    (cocky)

I like it!

                    MARY

If you act up Rosie, you'll be out. Master won't stand for
any cheeky nonsense.

Mary takes the envelope from her.

                    MARY

Anyway, Master is busy. You can't see him now. *(Pause)*
You know, Rosie . . . you shouldn't bother him too
much.

Rosie smiles, ironically.

                    ROSIE

Yes, ma.

52   EXT. COURTYARD—DAY

*The fish vendor comes to the servants quarters looking for Abraham.
Mary chases behind him.*

                    VENDOR

Abraham? Gone home?

                    MARY

I'm now in charge. From now on you must see me.

In Abraham's room, a small room off the courtyard, Theresa sits on

Abraham's bed while he busies himself making tea.

THERESA

And we always have to take the ferry there because it's on the other side of the canal. I don't like to go anymore but she forces me.

Mary looks up and sees Theresa. Her eyes narrow.

MARY

Eh! Treesa! Mummy's calling you.

Theresa pretends not to hear. Mary starts walking up the steps.

THERESA

I thought Mummy went out.

MARY
(sharp)

She's *here*. Upstairs. Go and see.

Reluctantly, Theresa comes down the rickety staircase.

MARY

You musn't go and sit like that. Not nice. Go inside your room now. How many times I told you not to go there?

THERESA
(angry)

I'm doing my homework.

Mary marches up the stairs. Abraham is making a pot of tea on a small gas burner. Some (Hindi) film music is playing on the radio. A small charpoy sits in the corner. He looks up warily as Mary comes in. She looks around carefully.

MARY

Madam knows the child is sitting with you like this?

ABRAHAM

What? You're starting all the time with me. This is not your place. Please go down.

MARY

Madam knows?

78

ABRAHAM

There's nothing. She brings her work and does.

MARY

I'll tell Madam. I know who you are, Abraham. I know your butler type. All the men are like this only. You think because you worked with Madam before that you can do what you like now!

ABRAHAM
(angry)

Don't make trouble.

She looks at him, his lungi revealing bare feet and a glimpse of his calfs.

MARY

Showing legs and all! Oh, Abraham. I'll show you something. Let me show you.

Mary lifts her arms and starts to do a strange and seductive snake dance. She finally stops, out of breath, laughing at Abraham's shocked reaction.

53   INT. MACINTOSH HOUSE—DAY

Lily sits at a roll-down desk with a pot of tea wearing a lovely floral print dress. She looks quintessentially English. Even the papers scattered everywhere, several cups of tea, a plant, could belong in an English country house. Lily looks longingly at the baby, who is in a cot next to her. Mary is still upset and avoids looking Lily in the eye. She shakes her head with an angry wounded expression, making Lily nervous.

MARY

Powder, Madam. Some more soap too.

LILY

I thought we just bought soap, where could it have gone?

Mary shoots an angry look at Abraham, who comes in with a handful of receipts and some fresh tea.

LILY

Thank you, Abraham.

He nods.

ABRAHAM

What for dinner, Madam?

LILY

In a minute.

As soon as he is out of earshot, Mary bends forward,

MARY
(whispering, conspiratorial)

Madam, I don't like to say, Madam, but Theresa is spending too much time with that man.

LILY

What are you talking about?

MARY

She's all the time in the servants quarters. It's not nice, Madam. Young girl and all. And Madam, too many things are missing also.

LILY

What things?

MARY

From the larder, Madam. All kinda things. Too much sugar, Madam. Jam, lotion. Lots of things. I can't say how much.

LILY
(surprised)

But I've known Abraham and his family since I was a child.

MARY
(doubtful)

Yes, Madam.

LILY

Have you said anything to him directly?

MARY

Oh no! I can't say. He'll be fighting with me.

The baby starts to cry. Lily quickly reaches out to pick her up.

MARY

I'll take her, Madam. I've got it. She's so hungry now, Madam. Poor child.

That Abraham man doesn't like it when I go to the larder, Madam. Baba needs soap and powder and all. I feel shy, Madam. His hand is all the time inside that room, Madam.

Lily reaches for a pile of keys.

LILY

Take my keys then.

Mary hesitates.

MARY

No, Madam. I can't, Madam. Your house keys and all.

LILY
(urging)

Go on! Take them.

MARY

No, no, Madam.

Mary's hand reaches out. She examines them, holding them carefully in her hand, then clasps her fingers tightly over her conquest.

MARY

Thank you, Madam. Thank you.

54   INT. ROSIE'S HOUSE—DAY

Rosie is putting on make-up. She is beautifully dressed in a turquoise-coloured dress with a chiffon scarf falling around her shoulders, her long hair coiled against her neck.

She applies a lip pencil to accentuate her mouth. An older hand (her mother's) reaches over to wipe some of it off. Rosie slaps the hand away.

ROSIE

Leave it, ma.

Gwen looks behind Rosie in the mirror. She scowls.

GWEN

You going to drive him away. Then what will you do?

ROSIE

What do you know about anything?

GWEN

What do I know? I know, I know. I had everything when was I your age. You have one chance and you're going to spoil it and end up with nothing.

ROSIE

Go and lie down, ma.

GWEN

You think you're alone, that you can do whatever you like?

Rosie turns to her, angrily.

ROSIE

Jealous . . .

Gwen laughs uncontrollably and almost chokes on her betel nut. A stream of red juice falls on the floor.

GWEN

I feel so sorry for you.

Rosie continues brushing her hair, still looking in the mirror. Gwen fixes her gaze on something outside the window. Rosie finally stands up, slipping on her shoes.

GWEN

Where are you going?

Rosie doesn't answer. She bangs the door shut.

GWEN
(shouting)

Jungly . . .!

55   EXT. CANAL—DAY (THAT AFTERNOON)

John sits at the back of a boat going along an inland canal. He is alone in the boat except for the boatman. He points to the end of a quay where a woman is waiting.

JOHN

Stop there.

The boat hovers near the edge and John holds out his hand for the woman to step in. As the boat winds its way down the canal, villagers watch the couple as they float along the water.

In the distance the ruins of a small abandoned church sits in the middle of thick vegetation. The boat slowly comes to a stop and John leads Rosie across the field. Hesitating, she stops and turns away.

ROSIE

I can't go with you, sir.

JOHN

You don't have to worry anymore. Forget everyone. They don't matter.

Emboldened, Rosie turns to John, her eyes wide with expectation. John strokes her luxurious hair, holding it in his hands, pressing his face to her waist. He pulls her around, kissing her, undressing her, until they fall to the ground.

56   INT. DARTINGTON SCHOOL FOR GIRLS—DAY (THE AFTERNOON)

From high overhead we look down on a roomful of young Indian girls, who are bent over a neat row of wooden desks.

Theresa is the only European. At the front of the room a teacher in a pink sari stands behind a small electric fan. This is a science class in the 3rd standard. The teacher points to a diagram of the human body. As she points the children chant.

CHILDREN
(chorus)

Heart, lungs, stomach. Heart, stomach, lungs.

TEACHER

Very nice. Heart is for . . .?

CHILDREN
(chorus)

Pumping blood.

TEACHER

Lungs are for? Who can tell me? Treesa must be knowing.

The teacher smiles encouragingly at Theresa. The other girls look at Theresa with some resentment. One girl in particular glares at her.

GIRL

Teacher's pet.

THERESA

The lungs take in air and blow up like balloons.

TEACHER
(impressed)

Very nice!

Pleased, the teacher rings a hand bell. The class is over.

57   INT. MACINTOSH HOUSE—DAY

Theresa is lying in bed, her face to the wall. Mary comes in, throwing the door open. She opens the curtains. The hot sun streams in. Upset and angry from the previous day, Theresa doesn't move.

MARY

Arre! What happened. See what time it is. What about school?

THERESA

I'm not going to school. I don't feel well. Can you call Mummy? I want to see Mummy.

MARY

Not well! What, stomach pain?

Theresa nods.

MARY

I told you. See what a dirty fellow. Whole house is suffering. He's making everyone sick.

Abraham putters around the kitchen and does his morning duties. His age and a stiff leg make him awkward; shuffling, puffing, as he empties out a container of water. The kitchen door suddenly swings open and Mary glares at him, her eyes on fire.

MARY

Madam's calling you.

Alarmed, he wipes his large worn hands on a dish towel and pushes a few strands of loose hair off his face.

Lily is sitting at the dining room table in a rose-printed silk dressing gown, her whole demeanour sober and distant. Abraham gives her a wide grin.

ABRAHAM

Morning, Madam.

LILY

Abraham, Theresa says she isn't feeling well and Mary thinks she may have eaten some bad food. I hope it wasn't anything from the house.

ABRAHAM
(surprised and worried)

No Madam, everything is boiled here. Kitchen is clean. Shall I make some tea for baby? Nice milky tea?

LILY

Yes, why don't you do that.

We see the edge of Mary's figure return to the kitchen like a predatory ghost. Worried, Abraham shuffles back into the kitchen. Mary is standing over the counter and looking down at a speck of dirt. She points at the dirt accusingly.

MARY

Look here. I'll make the tea . . .

She points to the stain again—something barely noticeable.

MARY

Look at this!

85

ABRAHAM
(angry)

Eh, ayah, what kind of business is this? What do you want with me? You've been after me since the beginning.

She opens and shuts the cupboards, pulling out all the cups and plates, pointing to more imaginary 'dirt' in the corner. Then she pulls out a handful of knives and forks, holding them up, turning them around, then throwing some on the counter.

MARY

What about this? Look here. Everyone will get sick with this. All the cutlery. Each and everyone with dirty marks.

Furious, Abraham reaches out and grabs at the cutlery she has thrown on the counter. He holds out a knife to show her how clean it is.

ABRAHAM

Everyday I wash this cutlery, twice, three times a day. Then I dry, then I put into the cupboard. Every day for twenty-five years. What you say is . . .

Suddenly the kitchen door swings open and Lily looks around the corner, still waiting for the tea. She hesitates, seeing Abraham with the knife pointed at Mary, not sure what to think.

MARY

Look what this man does. See what kind of thing he's doing in this house.

LILY

Can you bring the tea, please.

59   INT. DINING ROOM—DAY

Theresa is sitting in her place. Mary puts the tea in front her.

THERESA

Where's Mummy?

LILY (O.S.)

I'm coming, darling. Drink your tea.

MARY
(talking aloud to herself)

Who is he to jump over my head? *(Mimicking Abraham's voice)* Good morning, Madam. How was the garden, Madam?

THERESA
(obviously upset)

What's wrong, Mary? Abraham didn't do anything.

Mary bangs the drawer shut and throws the silverware on the top.

MARY

Nothing's wrong. Mama Coothi wrong.

Theresa stares at Mary.

MARY
(to Theresa)

What are you looking at? Uh? God is watching you, Abraham.

The kitchen door swings open and Abraham brings in a teapot. He walks past Mary to Theresa.

THERESA

Hello Abraham!

He pours more tea into her cup.

ABRAHAM

Not feeling well?

THERESA

I'm all right now. I'm feeling much better.

MARY

Chi! Don't tell lies. You tell Mummy one thing, then make a fool out of me?

Lily walks back into the room.

THERESA
(almost in tears)

I'm not lying. I *do* feel much better now. I just had a stomach ache. But it's gone now.

Mary suddenly starts talking aloud, alternating between two different voices as though she were narrating a story.

MARY

I said, Oh my God. She cut his hair? Really? She did it? Oh yes . . . A small piece of hair. She tied it to a tree. And where did she tie it? Near the Adjar river. Why did she do it? Oh yes . . . To drive him mad. Abraham . . . Which Abraham? First Abraham. And the wind from the river, the Adjar river was blowing his hair on the tree. Blowing and blowing until he became mad . . . mad . . .

LILY

What are you talking about, Mary?

MARY

Mad, mad, mad . . .

LILY
(sharply)

Mary! Answer me.

MARY

Oh. Nothing, Madam. It's just a story some of those hilly people told me. Anyway, I'm just an uneducated, Madam. What do I know to talk . . . I can't speak English properly.

Abraham stands next to Theresa. They are all staring at Mary.

MARY

Madam, I'm telling you, the child is sick and must go to bed. How many times shall I tell you about this man?

She motions to Abraham.

MARY

He doesn't understand what is going on here.

LILY

I don't understand either. What is going on?

Mary starts to pound her head with her hand.

He's dirty. He uses same toilet hand for everything. He doesn't have our clean standards Madam, how can I do my job with this going on?

We can hear the baby crying from upstairs.

MARY

If she gets sick, your doctor told only. Any sickness and baby will go.

Lily looks at Abraham, who shakes his head, watching Mary.

MARY

And what about that child?

She points to Theresa.

MARY

She goes and sits with him in the servants quarters. Off hours, Madam. What kind of thing is that? Young girl. He musn't let her do like that. What are people going to say? No, no, Madam. This is very bad.

ABRAHAM

Please, Madam.

THERESA
(crying)

But Mummy, it's not Abraham! He didn't do anything. Please don't be angry with him. Please, Mummy.

Torn and distressed, Lily looks at Abraham who looks back angrily at Mary, his hand shaking as he picks up the pot of tea.

LILY

Abraham, I think you had better get back into the kitchen. Theresa is sick and you shouldn't be playing with her.

ABRAHAM

Yes, Madam.

A young girl sits beneath a spindly pair of legs covered with thick coffee-coloured hose. Blossom's thick black shoes sit motionless against the wheelchair. The girl struggles to tie the long, waxy laces. The camera pans up to Blossom who is feeding the baby. She turns to Mary excitedly, disturbing the baby.

> BLOSSOM

Tell me, ma. Are you sure?

> MARY

I told you. Madam is coming on Wednesday. In two weeks. At four o'clock. Madam likes to have tea outside. *(Pause)* But keep your mind on the job, Blossom.

Blossom turns to look at the other Alms house women, sitting nearby on the veranda. Her whole face lights up.

> BLOSSOM

Harriet! Mina! Madam is coming! Sister, does Madam like fowl? Nothing with spice. Some boiled peas. And Mrs Mehta will give me a ham. I'm sure of it. Did you ask which one Madam prefers? Fowl or ham?

> MARY

Fowl.

> GWEN

You're so het up about Madam. No use to go to all this trouble. Just give a simple cup of tea.

> BLOSSOM
> *(offended)*

No, no. Madam must have a party. I will pull out the tablecloths and Mina, you should take out the good chairs. I'm going to wear my purple dress.

Suddenly self-conscious, she pulls at her skirt to try and hide her legs.

> BLOSSOM

You think she'll like that one, ma?

Lily is roused from a deep sleep in the middle of the day by the sound of coins dropping against the floor. John bends down to pick them up.

LILY

What time is it?

JOHN

Lunchtime, darling.

LILY

I couldn't really sleep. I've been so worried about everything. You came home so late.

JOHN

Rehearsals. We had a few drinks. That's all.

He shrugs, buttoning his shirt, then puts his keys in his pocket, getting ready to leave. He pulls out a nail clipper.

LILY

John, we haven't had time to talk about anything.

JOHN

I have to be on time today, Lily. I can't delay.

LILY

But John, I need to talk to you.

JOHN

We'll have a long talk when I get back.

LILY

John, I'm so confused. Maybe we should go back to England. Take baby to a proper doctor. We can find a flat in London. We can try again.

She caresses him and tries to kiss him. He stands up and moves away. Wounded, Lily moves to a corner of the bed.

JOHN

Look, why don't you try to rearrange things. Throw out some of this Indian stuff. You know, make the house look more like our old place.

He hurriedly tries to put everything into his bag. She watches him in a kind of daze and then, desperate for his help, reaches out again.

> LILY

John, I'm so worried about Abraham. Mary's been saying all sorts of dreadful things about him. I don't know what to do.

John comes toward the bed to kiss her.

> JOHN

What? Yes, of course I love you.

62   INT. MACINTOSH HOUSE—DAY (A DAY OR SO LATER)

Lily is alone at the table having breakfast. She seems numb. She taps the front of a soft-boiled egg and then lifts the top of the shell off the egg. It comes off in one piece.

Abraham starts to pour her some more tea. She covers her cup, her face downcast. Her voice is detached.

> LILY

No thank you, Abraham . . . I . . .

> ABRAHAM

Madam?

> LILY

Master is worried, and so am I, Abraham . . .

> ABRAHAM

Madam?

> LILY

There have been things missing from the house and it's not clean. I don't think we can keep you anymore.

Abraham puts down the pot of tea, his hand trembling a little bit. Lily tries not to see.

> ABRAHAM

But, Madam, I've never stolen even one spoon of sugar from this house.

LILY

Of course I'll give you excellent references.

Distressed, Lily looks at Abraham, his hands tucked behind his back, his face watching hers so intently. She looks defensive, trying to hide her guilty eyes.

LILY

I don't think you understand, Abraham. I can't afford to have the house in such a poor state.

ABRAHAM

She's against me since she came, Madam.

He looks toward the kitchen where Mary is peering through the porthole window.

LILY

Thank you, Abraham. I really can't discuss this. I'm sorry. We'll send your chits and things home.

Pause.

ABRAHAM

But, Madam. This is my home.

63   EXT. MAIDAN—DAY (SEVERAL DAYS LATER)

An expansive view of the Maidan. In the distance we see shapes emerging and then a swarm of ayahs and a fusion of colour. As they get close we hear the buzzing sound of their chatter . . . They all sit down, pulling out their snacks and bottles of drink. Mary has nodded off, one arm resting against the baby's carriage. Sleepy from the sun, Theresa sits quietly watching the other children.

AYAH 1

Are you sleeping, Mary ma?

MARY

I'm just closing my eyes. Slee-e-p, sle-e-ep, I'll sleep when I'm there.

She points upwards. The woman admires Mary's pink and white chequered dress.

What a beautiful dress, Mary. You bought it?

MARY

Madam just threw it.

One little girl with a complaint wanders sadly towards her ayah. Busy with her friends, the ayah pushes her away.

AYAH 3

Eh! Don't come to me now. Let me have a rest!

The girl doesn't really know what to do. The ayah turns to her friends.

AYAH 4

No! Changlepat-Madam has four bedrooms. I've seen the house, very modern. They make good money . . .

The girl wanders back and starts to cry.

AYAH 3

Leave me for five minutes, uh?

She gives her a push.

AYAH 3

Go on! All spoiled children, uh . . . See! Look over there!

She points to a large abandoned building across the park. It looks like a mausoleum or a tomb.

AYAH 3

I'll put you in there if you're naughty. Lots of Muslim spirits inside, they'll catch you and poke your eyes out!

The girl cries harder.

AYAH 5

See what Rosie's doing! Mother was same. I always say, what mother will do, child will also do.

The others murmur, trying not to let Mary hear.

MARY

Eh! Don't talk badly! Rosie is working in the hospital.

94

She's a very good girl.

The ayahs mutter to the contrary. Mary turns to Ayah 4.

MARY

Anyway, my Master has such a better house than your Madam's house.

She makes a face, grimacing at the thought.

MARY

In England. You know Wellington castle?

Everyone is quiet. They nod, pretending they do.

MARY

Near-to-there. He wants me to build a side house. Simple thing. Electric-city two-three rooms. Running water. But not now! Maybe three-four years.

Theresa stares at Mary and then at the ayahs as they click their tongues and move their eyes in circles of awe and disbelief.

Four women sitting very close to one another are whispering and giggling. One of them is telling a story. Mary leans in to hear. The camera pans around so that we see close-ups of their faces.

AYAH 7

He was so drunk. What could I do? You think this man listens to me? Madam is due to come home soon. He's shouting away in the kitchen and somebody told me . . . (you know, after) that they're getting his voice by the shop. Children are sleeping. It's nighttime you know. So finally I went into that kitchen . . . Oh, you can't believe it . . . No . . . You know what happened? . . .

Everyone shakes their head in suspense.

AYAH 7

. . . The bugger was wearing all of Madam's clothes.

The three others exclaim—amazed, covering their mouths, look horrified and then burst out laughing.

OTHER AYAHS

Wearing Madam's clothes! . . . What? All of Madam's clothes? Come on! Everything?

95

Everything!

OTHER AYAHS

Madam doesn't let us touch anything. We would never dare to do. We would never think to do.

AYAH 7

Oooh, I got so scared! What will Madam say? I wanted to tell him something but . . .

She gestures with her hand showing that he'd gone 'off'.

AYAH 2

And what happened? When Madam came?

The ayah rolls her eyes dramatically.

AYAH 7

Sacked! Then and there. Wearing Madam's shoes!

The others cluck, draw their heads in, laughing, then murmuring disapproval. An ayah stares suspiciously at Mary, looking her straight in the eye.

64   INT. MACINTOSH HOUSE—DAY

Mary is squatting in front of John's closet, her dress tucked between her legs as she finishes polishing another pair of John's shoes. The sound of a car horn distracts her.

She cranes her neck to see who it is. The chowkidar rushes to open the gate. A large black car rolls in. Two women, Joan and Anne, get out—both nurse-missionaries from an old English mission, wearing long loose uniforms. They are followed by Father Patrick, an Anglican minister. All three are wearing hats to shield their pale complexions from the sun.

Curious, she rushes downstairs, and opens the door.

MARY
(pleased)

Come in, come in please . . .

JOAN

Hello, is Mrs Macintosh here? Mrs Lily Macintosh . . .

She looks at Mary, and then speaks as if she isn't sure whether Mary understands English—enunciating her words slowly and precisely.

JOAN

We're nurses from St. Jude's. We've come to see Lily Macintosh and her baby. We always come round to see our new children. And we understand from Dr Correa that the child was early. We like to do an assessment and offer our recommendation to the new parents.

Joan repeats the word, hoping she's understood.

JOAN

Assessment . . .

MARY

Yes, yes . . . testing. Oh, I know. I was a nurse in Lady Wellington Hospital. I'll show you the child. Come in please. Let me see if Madam is here.

She bends her head and kisses the cross around her neck.

MARY

Reverend Father . . . Please come in, sir.

Excited, Mary leads them into the living room looking towards Lily's room upstairs.

ANNE

I know we've come unannounced. We're just in the area for a few days, back again next month.

MARY

Please, be my guest and have a seat. Tea will be coming. One second, please.

The three guests sit down while Mary goes upstairs. She goes to Lily's door—sees that she is fast asleep and gently but firmly closes the door. Excited, she rushes into her room to change and brush her hair before she collects the baby.

65   INT. LIVING ROOM—DAY

Mary sits in the centre of the room in a large upholstered armchair. She hands the tea around, urging them to have some.

97

MARY

Biscuits?

ANNE

Are you sure we shouldn't wait?

MARY
(nervous)

No, no. Madam told to start. Tea is getting cold and I'll
have to take the child soon for a rest. Please take it.

Joan blows a kiss to the baby, propped up on the couch.

JOAN

Oh, isn't she a luv. Look at her. Terribly thin, isn't she
Anne? How early was she, Mary?

MARY

Child was born seven months. I'm here since that time
nah.

JOAN

May I?

MARY

Please, Madam.

*Joan gently picks the baby up from the couch, then puts her next to
Father Patrick and begins to take down a few notes on a pad of paper.
Mary looks on impatiently, glancing upstairs nervously. To pass the
time she hands Anne the picture of her mother and father.*

MARY

Just to have a quick look. My father, an officer in the
British regiment and my mother at Ryaputah hospital.
Near to Jorbagh.

ANNE

Oh, how fascinating. 1 think I visited this place some
years ago. What's happened to it now?

Mary carefully sips her tea.

MARY

I don't know, Madam.

ANNE

Well, you must be a terrific help to Mrs Macintosh with the baby.

MARY

You see, Madam, I left the hospital to look after this child. I said, God, who's going to take care of her? I had a dream like that, you know.

ANNE

She's lucky to have someone as dedicated as you. How is Lady Wellington doing anyway? That's another place we visited. Back in '50. Donkeys ago.

MARY

You see, Madam. Before. I have to tell you. It was much better before the British left.

Amused, the nurses glance at one another.

JOAN

The place has deteriorated, it's true!

MARY

This child. She's my life now. There's nothing else. Mother, father, all is gone now. Only the child . . . my child . . .

Her eyes begin to fill with tears. She puts her face next to the baby, who gurgles happily, reaching out to touch her nose. The nurses exchange glances, touched but also concerned by Mary's extreme devotion.

Upstairs, awoken from a deep sleep by the sound of voices, Lily gets up. Hot and sweating, she pushes open the window to let in some fresh air. A gust of wind from the sea blows in.

Downstairs, Katy starts cleaning up as she hears sounds coming from Lily's room. She makes a motion to get up, pretending the baby is tired.

MARY

Poor child is getting so tired now. Time to go. Better
go.

JOAN

Oh, dear. We'll just be a minute longer. Has she had
any infection? That's quite common, you know. Any
chest cold?

MARY
(rushing)

Not one sick day. She's with me night and day.

JOAN

Have any idea how much she weighs? Probably not
very much, poor thing.

MARY

That I can't say, Madam. But she eats very well.

JOAN

Mrs Macintosh is breast-feeding her then?

Mary shakes her head, holding the baby near her breast.

MARY

I'm in charge of feeding.

They give her a second look, misunderstanding.

JOAN

Well, isn't that lucky! The two nurses and the Father
nod their heads together.

ANNE

A real miracle. Isn't that right, Father?

The Father nods.

FATHER

It's Mary?

MARY

Cotton Mary, Father.

Father Patrick looks at the cross around her neck.

FATHER

You have a strong faith I see.

MARY

Jesus said, Come all the little children unto me.

The Father smiles.

FATHER

Bless you, my child.

Mary kisses her cross. Joan hands a card to Mary.

JOAN

If you're ever in London, Mary, look us up. There's always an extra bed at the mission.

Unnoticed, Lily slowly descends the stairs in the background. She's still in her dressing gown.

MARY

Next time I'll be going to London to see the Queen! Who knows. God only knows. *(Pause)* Pussy cat, pussy cat, where have you been? I've been to London to see the Queen.

FATHER PATRICK
(taken aback)

Oh!

Lily is standing at the staircase.

FATHER PATRICK

Hello.

LILY

I'm Lily. Lily Macintosh.

The nurses beam at Mary undeterred.

JOAN

How very lucky to have such a person in your employ, Mrs Macintosh. How very lucky indeed. We've had a most wonderful tea.

FATHER PATRICK

No doubt God's hand has a role in it, Mrs Macintosh.

MARY

Some tea, Madam?

FADE OUT

ACT III

The Alms House

66   EXT. GARDEN/MACINTOSH HOUSE—DAY (SEVERAL DAYS LATER)

The sound of cooing—a hoopoe bird—it repeats.

The sharp blade of a sickle moves swiftly across a row of flowers. They fall to the ground. Joseph, Mary's cousin-brother and the new butler in training, roughly gathers them into a bouquet.

67   INT. MACINTOSH HOUSE—DAY

Mary is in the kitchen drinking her morning tea. Theresa is finishing up her breakfast, her book bag on her shoulder.

Joseph comes inside with the flowers. Mary shakes her finger at him.

MARY

You must cut more flowers. Flowers for all the house, not just Madam and Master's room. Understand?

He nods.

MARY

One minute.

She takes the key from around her neck and unlocks the larder. She presses a pack of English cigarettes into Joseph's hand. He takes it gratefully.

MARY
(entreating)

After cleaning, go and put special flowers for Master. Small small purple flower by the bedside. Okay?

Joseph nods. Theresa watches Joseph put down the flowers and pick up a silver bowl he is polishing. He lights up a cigarette. He has a dark untrustworthy air about him. Mary glares at him, suddenly displeased with his casual manner.

MARY

You know right-hand serving, nah?

Joseph nods.

But no talking. Only come when Madam calls. You can see everything from the window.

Joseph looks at the small round window, just big enough for a face.

MARY

For tonight Master likes double-whiskey soda water inside. Double-whiskey. No mistakes. Understand?

Joseph nods. The door opens and John peers his head around the corner and clears his throat, announcing his arrival at the breakfast table.

JOHN

Where's Mrs Macintosh?

MARY
(excitedly)

Madam's taken the car, sir. She's gone for a drive. I'm coming sir, coming, coming.

John sits down at the table and glances at the baby left in her pram and starting to cry. The noise makes it difficult for him to read. She cries even harder.

JOHN

Mary!

MARY (O.S.)

Coming.

Disturbed, he reaches out his hand to rock the pram while still trying to read. She thrashes about, screaming more. Muttering to himself, John covers her, then tries with some difficulty to take the baby out of the pram. He holds her awkwardly, at arm's length, as if he were frightened, and then looks away, still determined to read.

MARY
(seeing him with the baby)

Sorry, sir. Sorry. Sorry.

Mary rushes into the room with John's breakfast of eggs, sausage, toast and fried tomatoes.

68   INT. ALMS HOUSE—DAY (SAME MORNING)

An older woman's hand pins a delicate garland of jasmine and baby roses into the crown of Blossom's wavy, dark hair. The woman, Mattie, holds up a mirror.

MATTIE
(anxious)

Do you like it?

The flowers look as if they have been woven directly into her hair.

BLOSSOM

Thank you, Mattie, it's wonderful. But will it stay until Madam comes?

Mattie nods reassuringly and starts to clear the remaining pins. She cleans the comb and winds the loose fallen hair into a ball. Blossom reaches up and they clasp hands.

69   INT. MACINTOSH HOUSE—DAY

Mary unfolds a page from an English women's magazine—a photograph of women modelling short haircuts. She examines the cuts and circles one which is worn by a tall dark-haired model. Her hand reaches up to her own hair, folded into a tight bun.

Theresa comes into the kitchen with her bowl and looks over her shoulder.

THERESA
(suprised)

Are you going to cut your hair?

Mary quickly hides the photo in her pocket and pushes her away.

MARY
(angrily)

Go on! Go to school. All the time you're sneaking and peeking. Here and there. See what happens to you. Snake is going to come and get you. He's going to bite you.

Frightened, Theresa backs off and leaves for school. Just then the back door slams and the dhobi walks in with a newly pressed yellow dress.

Dress is ready . . .

Mary reaches out her hand.

MARY

I'll take it. I'm going upstairs.

The dhobi gives her a strange look, and then shrugs, wanting no part of it. Joseph stands near the window and lights up another cigarette.

MARY
(To Joseph)

You do your duty, man. I have to take the child out till the afternoon. I don't know when Madam and Master are coming. Cousin-cousin, doesn't mean you don't have to work, uh?

She leaves the kitchen, the yellow dress hanging carefully from her arm.

70   INT. MARY'S ROOM—DAY

Mary slips her stockinged feet into a pair of white leather shoes belonging to Lily. They fit perfectly. She stands up in them and walks around. We hear the slip-slip sound of the leather against the tiled floor.

The baby gurgles from her carriage, thrusting her little hands out in glee. Mary bends down to adjust the fancy lace collar around her neck . . .

MARY

Yes, darling . . .

. . . then checks herself in the mirror. She lifts the same freshly pressed yellow dress up to tighten the thick band around her waist. The result is transforming, giving her a new, flat shape. Pleased, she moves the dainty leather handbag she has procured from Lily over her wrist, pushes the baby's carriage and walks out the door.

71   EXT. KONDICHETTI MARKET—DAY

The mid-morning sun is already searing hot. People in the marketplace seek relief under shaded areas. Vendors cover their fruit and vegetables with wet cloths. At a taxicab stand, the drivers rest in the cool shade provided underneath the cars. As Mary walks proudly through the streets, people look up from their respective posts—curious about her appearance.

72   INT. BUTCHER'S—DAY

A small grimy shop, with animal parts (lungs, kidneys, etc.) openly displayed from the sides and the ceiling. Flies sit freely over the meat. Mary covers her nose from the smell. She puts a handkerchief over the baby's face to protect her from the flies. The butcher is pleased to see her.

> BUTCHER

Ah! Cotton Mary. Good morning ma. You're looking so nice, Mary, like . . . like a proper memsahib! Meat is all ready for you!

He reaches up to a shelf and pulls down a package. He opens the paper, grinning.

> BUTCHER

Very hard to find this!

Mary stares into it. At a closer look, we see a huge tongue lying flat against the paper. Mary looks dubious.

> BUTCHER
> *(reassuring her)*

Best one. Sahib will love it!

Mary nods. He wraps it up again.

> MARY

This is Master's favourite. This and fish curry!

The butcher smiles. Mary flicks her hand to say goodbye.

73   INT. MACINTOSH HOUSE—DAY

The house seems unusually dark and quiet. Lily looks into the children's room. Two of her dresses and a pair of her shoes lie scattered across the floor. Someone is crying.

> LILY

Theresa?!

Theresa is sitting in the corner by the bed, arms wrapped around her knees and crying.

Darling? Why aren't you at school?

Lily is suddenly struck by how thin and frightened she looks.

LILY

Where's Mary and the baby? Why are you all alone?

Unconsolable, Theresa remains in the same position. Lily sits down beside her and begins to smoothe her hair.

LILY

It's all right, darling. You don't need to be afraid.

She moves closer and tries to hold Theresa, folding her tightly into her arms.

THERESA
(angry)

You just want her to stay because of the baby. All you care about is the baby.

LILY

I care about you, darling, so much.

THERESA

You can't even feed her. You don't even care that she takes us to her sister's house.

LILY

Takes you where, my darling? What are you saying?

THERESA

All those horrible old ladies just staring at me. And her sister's in a wheelchair.

LILY

Who's in a wheelchair?

THERESA

Mary's sister. She's the one feeding the baby.

Lily holds Theresa, and tries to keep her calm. She holds her in her arms and speaks very slowly, trying to reassure her.

LILY

Darling, Mummy tried to feed the baby but I couldn't so
I asked Mary to help me. The baby was very sick.

THERESA

What about Abraham? Why can't Abraham come back?
He didn't do anything. You should never have fired
him. He was my friend. This is his house too.

*Lily looks at Theresa, seeing the depth of her response. She hesitates,
allowing herself to realize what she has done. She tries to embrace
her, but Theresa pulls back.*

LILY
(slowly)

I know. I've made a terrible mistake. I'm sorry.

THERESA

Daddy's gone and now Abraham's gone too. It's all
your fault.

Lily watches helplessly as tears stream down Theresa's face.

74   EXT. MALABAR HOTEL—DAY

*A large stately hotel patronized by tourists, foreigners and wealthy
locals. Two porters in decorative dress stand on either side of a
revolving door.*

*A car drives up and several elegantly dressed Europeans get out. Mary
tries to follow directly behind them, holding the baby in her arms. The
porters nod respectfully at the baby and, consequently, allow Mary to
pass.*

75   INT. MINNIE'S BEAUTY SHOP—DAY

*A sign (Minnie's Beauty Shop) hangs overhead. Mary goes inside
pushing the carriage first. The receptionist, a fair-skinned Anglo-Indian
of another—higher—class, glances up from the appointment book.
She seems apprehensive.*

RECEPTIONIST
(cold)

Yes?

Mary looks at a long mirror in which rows of women at various stages

109

of hairstyling are reflected. The women are mostly European. They stare back at her, their expressions a mixture of curiosity and disdain.

MARY

Minnie?

The receptionist ignores her for a few moments.

RECEPTIONIST

Are you looking for someone?

Stylists in identical pink coats are whispering to one another in the corner. Mary stands taller.

MARY

A trim please. Something like this.

She pulls out the magazine picture and shows it to her.

RECEPTIONIST

One minute please.

Another customer, an Englishwoman, comes into the shop. She takes one look at Mary.

WOMAN

Excuse me . . . Is this the right place? Sorry, I must have the wrong salon . . .

The receptionist's voice is now markedly different.

RECEPTIONIST

No, no. Please come in, Madam. Take a seat.

MARY

I have a lunch appointment. Don't take too much time miss.

Taken aback, both the receptionist and the customer give Mary a second look. The receptionist calls one of the stylists.

RECEPTIONIST
(whispering)

She's not a normal ayah. I don't know who she is.

STYLIST

Better give her a chair. You never know.

110

They discuss it. The stylist looks at Mary and points to an empty chair.

RECEPTIONIST

Come with me, please.

Mary sits down, pushing the baby's carriage into the corner. The receptionist gestures to Mary's hair in the mirror.

RECEPTIONIST

Trim.

The stylist nods, looking at Mary in the mirror.

STYLIST
(hesitant)

Some coffee or tea for you miss?

MARY

No thank you.

STYLIST
(looking at photograph)

You like the shorter look, then? Yes, I think it will suit you. It always gives a young and fresher look. Most of our clients are wearing shorter styles these days.

Mrs Davids and Mrs Evans (who we saw in Lily's garden) have been staring at Mary. They look away and begin talking to one another in the mirror. Their stylists stand behind them, as they do or undo a few curlers.

MRS DAVIDS
(eyes narrowing)

Of course it's her. I recognized her immediately. She's the one looking after the baby.

MRS EVANS
(genuine disbelief)

I just can't believe she's in here. Look what she's wearing. Lily's dress, and my dear, her white leather shoes.

MRS DAVIDS

This is what comes of a free hand. I warned Lily. Look at the result. There's no turning back now.

111

I'm coming, Mrs Evans!

A poster of an Indian model with voluptuous thick black hair is right above her. A small boy comes around with a tray of tea and Nescafé coffee.

RECEPTIONIST

Is everything all right, Mrs Evans? Your colour's coming in so nicely today.

At another station, the stylist moves Mary's head to face the mirror. Her hair is shorter but not by much. Mary glances at the photo on her lap.

MARY

You can cut some more.

STYLIST

As you like, miss.

She takes a large handful of Mary's hair.

76   EXT. ALMS HOUSE—DAY

Mattie pushes Blossom's chair through the house, which is busy and pulsing with activity. A group of women in the corner are making decorations with coloured paper. Blossom's eyes move excitedly around the room. She tries to repress a smile which, moments later, spreads openly, childishly, across her face.

Suddenly three small girls rush in with a plate of food.

GIRLS

Tasting please!

BLOSSOM

Come here then! Quickly!

LUCY

Be careful girls! Careful of the dress, child. Give it to me, let me press it now.

The girls watch eagerly for Blossom's reaction. Blossom takes a piece of the sweet, caramel-covered cake off the tray.

BLOSSOM

Sticky toffee!

112

Will Madam like it?

BLOSSOM
(laughing excitedly)

Of course! It's delicious. Madam will love it.

77   INT. MINNIE'S SALON—DAY

Mary is still listening to the same women while the stylist blow-dries her hair. A wealthy Parsi lady is sitting under the dryer, her eyes darting back and forth across the room.

MRS DAVIDS

They'll never get rid of her now.

MRS EVANS

Gracious! Look what she's done to her hair. What's she up to?

MRS DAVIDS

She better not come anywhere near me. I'll have a word or two.

MRS EVANS

She's here with the baby, for Godsakes.

MRS DAVIDS
(sniffing)

What's that dreadful smell? Something rancid. It's coming from over there. Near her. Something's rotting.

The word travels. One by one all the other women at the mirror turn and hold their noses and smell something awful.

STYLIST
(unsure)

It's from outside, Madam.

Mary looks around tentatively (her hair is shorter and 'coiffed' like the other ladies now). She reaches down to the baby carriage and slowly pulls out the bag of meat from a side pocket.

She unwraps it just halfway, and smells it again. The women look at the tongue—it lies flat against the paper and out of the butcher shop it looks almost surreal.

113

Who is she?

The tongue is almost a purplish colour in the fluorescent light. Mary stands to face her neighbours. She has a certain stature with her new hair, her dress, etc. The women are confused.

MARY

Mary, Madam. Cotton Mary. Who wants to know . . .

MRS DAVIDS

Tell her to be quiet!

MARY

Everyone has to talk. You can't shut me up. My father was in the British regiment, Madam. What's the difference? Because I'm black you talk to me like this?

The women look faint. Mary takes the tongue, holding the thick triangular slab of meat with both hands and confronts the women— threatening them, dangling it dangerously close to their faces for them to smell.

MARY

Come on, Madam, smell. what kind of smell is there? Go on. Take it and see.

Horrified, the women move back, turning away, feeling sick. Mary throws the tongue next to the cash register and looks contemptuously at the room of women staring at her in utter disbelief.

MARY

See. No smell is coming now.

WOMAN

Good God. Get her out of here.

Confusion follows. Several women get up, apparently disoriented and frightened by the chaos Mary is generating. Minnie, the patroness, takes Mary by the arm, asking her to leave in a hushed voice. The stylists fan out among their customers, reassuring them that the crisis has passed.

78 EXT. MARKET—DAY

Lily leads Theresa through a maze of small huts at the edge of the

114

local market located at an intersection of canals. People stare at them. Someone pushes against her accidentally. But she makes her way as if she knows exactly where she is going. Theresa looks around, completely confused.

THERESA

Where are we, Mummy? Where are we going?

Lily stares ahead and grips Theresa's hand. She points to an old run down building, long past its prime, with skinny, tired-looking children crawling across the entrance towards a dog.

LILY

That's where Abraham used to live.

THERESA
(calling out, excited)

Abraham! Abraham!

Theresa races ahead before Lily can catch her, shouting out his name, racing ahead into the building and up the stairs.

Lily follows Theresa tentatively, climbing the dark and dirty staircase leading up to the top floor. She stops at the top to look down at the view—people thronging the market, traffic choking the street. The contrast to the subdued beauty of Lily's house is dramatic. Theresa tugs her arm impatiently, pulling her down the hallway.

THERESA
(urgently)

Come on, Mummy!

At the end of a dingy hallway, there is the sound of frying foods and the high pitched wail of a love song on the radio. Suddenly anxious, Lily moves slowly towards a room at the back. We hear the sound of voices. Lily peers tentatively into the room.

LILY

Abraham?

A family of six or seven sit eating their midday meal. Everyone looks up, astonished.

LILY

Abraham? Is Abraham here?

The man and woman confer with one another.

115

Abraham's not living here since long time.

LILY

But this was his mother's place. She had all her things
here.

MAN

Mother's dead. Abraham lives near—Kandichetti Road.
One big house is there. He is living there.

*He gestures to the stark room to indicate Abraham's absence as they
start to resume their meal.*

79   INT. THE ALMS HOUSE—DAY

*The Alms house women wearing their best dresses and saris are
gathered around Blossom, beginning to doze off. Several small fans
blow air from side to side. Everyone is tired of waiting. Some of the
villagers rock their babies on home-made hammocks.*

WOMAN 1
(whispering)

I don't think she's coming. We'll go home then . . . the
child is too tired now.

WOMAN 2
(fed up)

Yes, those people are usually so punctual.

*Blossom waves her hand over the sandwiches, covered with a delicately
crocheted dolly. A group of flies scatter. She looks at the Oriental rug
laid out as a welcome mat for Lily and the table inside—with flowers
and linen napkins folded decoratively into the glasses.*

*She spreads her dress over her knees, trying to flatten out some new
wrinkles. A fly settles on her hand. She slaps it away—she's agitated
and hot. Mira comes running with a fly-swatter.*

BLOSSOM

Mira, bring some nimbu for the guests. You can serve
the sandwiches too. They'll be coming any minute
now. Come, Gwen, come and sit down with me.

Embarrassed, Gwen moves into a corner of the veranda, squeezed

116

between several other women.

GWEN

I can see Madam from here only. You must talk to her.
You must stay in front.

*The servant-girl begins to serve the sandwiches when she sees Mary
approach. A puzzled expression gradually changes to recognition. She
runs to Blossom excitedly, pointing to the road.*

GIRL

They're here! Madam is coming!

*Everyone suddenly perks up. Women straighten their clothes, the
babies are whisked into their arms. A woman rushes back to the
kitchen to heat a pot of food.*

BLOSSOM

The flag!

*A boy darts out from the house and proudly holds out the Union Jack.
One woman is so excited at this 'raising' of the flag that she begins to
cry. The others clap, overwrought. The other women also begin to cry.*

*The street is full of people and Blossom searches through the crowd
until she sees Mary and the baby approach. She pauses at Mary's
appearance and has to refocus her eyes; Mary's new haircut, the bright
custard yellow colour of her dress, her patent leather shoes, the
stockings, her slow, unhurried gait.*

*Eventually, she allows herself to search for Lily. Her eyes move
hopefully across the street. The women look at one another nervously.*

WOMAN

Any minute, any minute now . . .

*Blossom closes her eyes. A slight breeze cools her face. Long pause
Mary steps into the compound alone. She moves slowly across the
floor, looking at Blossom.*

MARY

Sister, what a beautiful dress!

*She stretches out her arms, taking in the table laden with food, the tray
of drinks, the Alms house women wearing their starched cotton
dresses. She sees Gwen carefully watching her.*

117

Thank you so much! Please, eat. Eat and enjoy yourself!

The women all look at one another, whispering, confused.

A low murmur goes through the veranda. The disappointment is visible. The women turn to one another and begin to talk. They look at Blossom, waiting to see her reaction.

Mary hands Baba to her sister. Blossom's hands tremble as she takes the child. She turns her wheelchair away, her expression hard, resolute, as she realizes what has happened.

Mary strides across the room.

MARY

Please! Let's begin the feast.

No one moves.

MARY

What? Who's waiting for Madam? Raise your hand . . . I say everybody must eat.

The women back away. Blossom moves slowly toward Mary in her wheelchair. As she speaks, her voice is full of anger.

BLOSSOM
(quietly)

Before, you know, I had so many other children. You remember. Madam always came to see me. But I don't know why so many weeks, this Madam is not coming. I'm taking much care, and still, I didn't get nothing.

She shakes her head, becoming angrier.

MARY
(resentfully)

What, nothing? Madam sent so many beautiful things!

Blossom dismisses her comment, speaking louder and more forcefully.

BLOSSOM

People are asking me, sister, where is the mother? What does she look like, this Madam? They say, 'Whose child is this?' 'Where is the child's mother?' The child who comes here everyday. *(Pause)* What shall I tell them, sister?

Mary gets up, angrily.

MARY

What do you care what people say? Do your job and that's all, what?

Mary looks around the veranda, hoping to see some support.

MARY
(indignant)

She wants something from Madam! Like what? It's not enough to bring Baba here, she still wants something more . . . uha . . . What more? Mama Coothi more.

She pauses, looking at her sister. She shakes her head in disbelief.

MARY
(mocking)

That world is dead and gone, sister. You can sit and wait like a bundocks. Madam will never come! Those days are past, sister . . . You're living in dreamland, darling.

MARY

What for you need Madam?

She spits onto the floor and shows her keys in a coarse, crude way.

MARY

Modern times, sister. Mr Gandhi's come and gone. How long you going to wait?

She begins to laugh. The older women in the group look noticeably shocked. One or two begin to cry. Another one glances at the portrait of the Queen Mother hanging inside the common room. She crosses herself. Several others go into the room to pray.

BLOSSOM
(pious)

God is with us in this place, sister. We may be poor but we have our self-respect.

The women nod, agreeing with Blossom. Mary spins around.

119

MARY

What do you want? . . . Money?!

She thrusts her hand into her pocket.

MARY
(hatefully)

Here! Take it.

She throws rupee bills and change onto the ground. The money spills across the floor near Blossom's feet. The camera slowly moves up from Blossom's feet across her legs over the baby in her lap to her face—contorted with rage.

BLOSSOM

I am not the prostitute to take money from you like that.

She takes a long breath.

BLOSSOM

Go and look for your Master. He's with your friend Rosie. See what your Master does with that woman! See which times have changed. Open your eyes, sister . . .

Mary shakes her head, shocked and confused. She sways, as if she could fall, as if the wind had been knocked out of her. There's a silence all around. Everyone is watching. Mary turns, her anger refuelled.

MARY
(to everyone)

Whoooo dares to talk about my Master like this?

Mary plants herself in the centre of the veranda. Her eyes are fiery, they dart around the room as if she were accusing and challenging everyone at once.

MARY

Whoooo dares to talk like this about an Englishman, a man like our own father?

She points to Blossom.

MARY

What are you? Just a crippled thing. Anglo-Indian

crippled thing. Worth nothing! You need Madam to come so everyone can see who you are—half-caste girl with no legs.

Tears roll down Blossom's face. She tears the baby away from her breast.

BLOSSOM
(Her voice is trembling)

Take her.

The crowd is still.

MARY
(dismissive)

What are you talking about?

BLOSSOM
(shouting)

Take her!

She wheels herself next to Mary and almost throws the baby into her sister's hands. Then she summons all her strength to wheel herself out of the room. Her brow is covered with sweat as she manoeuvers her chair across the floor. Anguished, she begins to laugh.

BLOSSOM
(bitter)

Father? What father? Your father, Captain in the British army! Your Captain father was nothing more than a poor bastard shining British shoes.

The door slams shut. Mary trembles, her face contorted with anger, her eyes bloodshot and wide with fear. She looks around furiously for another target.

MARY

It's that girl, Rosie. She's the one. She's always been like that, from the time she was a child watching her mother.

Gwen stares hard at Mary, the bitterness evident on her face.

GWEN

My Rosie hasn't done anything that she should be ashamed of. One day, she's going to leave this place.

She will do it. I have taught her how.

80   INT. ROSIE'S HOUSE—DAY

Viewed from a distance, Mary is one of many walking through the bazaar pushing the baby's pram. Peering over Rosie's shoulder, John strains to see. He leans further to the left. Partly obscured by stalls selling vegetables, Mary suddenly disappears and then reappears in an open stretch. John stands half-naked at the window, watching her.

JOHN

Jesus Christ! That's Mary.

He jumps out of the way. Rosie presses herself against John's chest, kissing him, caressing him, wrapping him with her long hair. She watches her friend and then turns away, as if she didn't want to see her.

ROSIE

(casually)

Hah jee. Mary's sister, my Blossom Auntie, lives in the Alms house. My Auntie is feeding your Baba.

She runs her finger seductively across his chest and undoes the shirt she is wearing to reveal her breast. She offers it to John, urging him on. Kissing her, he inches his way down.

ROSIE

Madam's milk was no good. So, Baba takes her milk over there.

Angrily, he suddenly pushes her away roughly.

JOHN

Get off. What the hell are you talking about?

81   EXT. ROSIE'S HOUSE—DAY

John slams the back door just as a group of village children run behind Mary as she approaches the front gate. Mary sees John from a distance. She waves furiously and calls after him. Her voice is raw and anguished.

MARY

Master! Master!

122

Incredulous, Mary beats on Rosie's door and pulls it open. It sticks. She has to pull harder.

MARY

Rosie! It's Cotton Mary. What have you done, Rosie? Come out! I want to see you, Rosie. God is with me.

She starts to cry. She steps closer. The room is dark.

Some of the children have followed her into the house. A curtain separates the bed from the main room. Mary hesitates and then pulls it open. She jumps back, seeing Rosie naked in the bed.

MARY

Oh God . . .

Rosie sits up and swings her head around forcefully, her hair spreading across her naked body. Rosie's expression is savage, angry and then she suddenly begins to laugh at Mary's stunned and childish reaction.

ROSIE

Poor Mary ma, doesn't know what to say. She thinks everyone should keep quiet and listen to the Master. 'Say your prayers Rosie, don't be cheeky, Rosie. Don't spoil your name, Rosie.' You want to check me now? I can do anything, Mary. Nobody cares anymore. Not even your precious Master.

Mary turns around and runs out of the house, talking to herself as she looks at the children, dazed and disoriented, clutching her chest furiously.

MARY

What happened?! Oh, God . . . Oh, God . . . Oh Jesus . . .

82   EXT. MACINTOSH GARDEN—DAY

From up in the tree, Theresa can see the traffic, and hear the slow pulsing sound of a bicycle wheel, the rickety creaking of rickshaws. She is without expression, sitting still, her gaze vacant. Below, a horn honks impatiently. The gate squeaks as the chowkidar runs to open it, saluting. John gets out of the car and slams the door. A moment later he is marching across the garden towards Lily.

JOHN
(indignant)

What the hell has been going on here? Where's the baby?

LILY

She's with Mary. Why?

JOHN

Why didn't you tell me you were sending her to some filthy woman on the street?

LILY

What are you talking about?

JOHN
(exploding)

Handing over the baby to be fed by some sort of prostitute, some bloody half-breed in an Alms house.

Lily pauses, then turns away.

LILY
(angrily)

How dare you question me like this? It was the only hope I had.

JOHN

Don't be ridiculous.

LILY

I couldn't feed her. Do you understand that?

JOHN

You could have asked our friends, you could have asked the bloody doctor.

LILY

You wouldn't even speak with the doctor.

JOHN

You've neglected your children, Lily.

LILY
(bitter)

Is that what they say about me at the club? What else
do they say, John? Do they talk about all your trips
around India? Do they ask why you stay away so long?
How we manage for such long stretches when we're
apart?

John turns to leave.

JOHN

It's not India, Lily. You know that. It's not India.

83   INT. MACINTOSH BEDROOM—NIGHT

*Theresa watches as her mother moves back and forth across the
room, watching for Mary. The chowkidar sits outside, smoking and
chatting with Mary's cousin, Joseph. There is no movement in the dark,
dimly lit street. Suddenly, Lily turns sharply to Theresa.*

LILY
(To Theresa)

Come on, I want you in bed. It's late.

84   INT. LIVING ROOM—NIGHT

*As the two of them go upstairs Mary enters, followed by Joseph. Dead
drunk, he collapses into an armchair. Mary tightens the cloth around
her head and ties it in a knot. There is a raw, disturbed quality to her.
Her eyes are swollen from crying, her hair is tousled.*

MARY

Do whatever you want. Master is gone. Madam is
upstairs sleeping. No one to care, man.

He blocks his ears from the sound of the baby's hungry cry.

JOSEPH
(thick drunken voice)

Is the baby sick?

Several bottles of milk sit on the table—untouched.

MARY

She's fine. She has to get used to it now. Oh, Madam!

Lily rushes downstairs, her face drawn and angry. She picks up the baby, who stops crying to cough.

LILY
(icy)

What's going on? Where've you been? It's almost ten o'clock. Why is she coughing? Is she sick?

Mary shrugs.

MARY

I'm sick now Madam, leave me alone. We're not your servants every minute, nah? India is a free country now, Madam.

Joseph stumbles up out of his chair. Lily moves back seeing how drunk he is.

JOSEPH

Like to have one drink, Madam?

LILY

Get him out of here.

Mary shrugs.

MARY

Don't take any notice. She likes to shout at the servants like this. They're all like that. He-ee acts like a big man—British-yes-sir-no-sir man. Shoes must be polished, shirts nicely pressed. Oh yes. Special breakfast. And what? He goes in the bed with that thing. No self-respect. Nothing! Chih-chih-chih. Underneath the ladies' petticoat . . .

She lifts up her own dress and makes a crude gesture, to illustrate.

MARY

Don't stand on one leg, Mummy, boys will think you're asking for what's underneath. All that bully-beet loudmouth, long-hair Rosie talk! Ah ah. Dirty bugger. Chih!

LILY

What are you talking about?

126

MARY
(muttering)

She doesn't know anything. Eyes are closed all the
time. That's good, keep your eyes closed, darling.
You'll sleep well, sweetheart. Better not to see.

*Lily looks at Mary, her clothes, her earrings, the chain around her neck.
She fixes on the chain. She comes closer.*

LILY

What's that around your neck?

MARY

You gave it to me, Madam.

LILY

What?

*Lily comes very close. She reaches out to touch it, then pulls her hand
back, not wanting to touch Mary.*

LILY

You took it from my room! Look at you, everything
you're wearing is mine.

MARY

What? You throw things away and then you come and
ask me . . . Open your eyes. Better go and look for your
husband. Find him first.

*Shocked and angry, Lily walks across the room and sits down with the
baby, who whimpers and cries.*

LILY

What have you done to my child?

MARY
(to Joseph)

Oho! Now she's blaming me only. If not for me your
child will be dead. Why to stay and get words. I don't
need to stay with you anymore. Let your husband take
care of you.

Lily stands up and walks to the door.

Get out. Take your things and go.

MARY

I'm going, Madam. You stay here alone, Madam. I'll go, Madam. I'll go.

As she turns to go she sees something moving in the corner.

MARY

Spying, uh? What you going to do? Tell Johnnie?

We see Theresa huddled against the staircase in the darkness, her little face peering through the wooden railing.

85 INT. MACINTOSH HOUSE—EARLY MORNING

Lily has been sitting with the baby through the night. The baby is crying in her arms; several half-empty bottles are on the table beside her.

Over and over she draws the baby towards her, kissing her forehead, her tiny hands. She buries her face in the warm cloth covering the baby's body and gently rocks her, overcome with emotion.

As the baby keeps crying, Lily walks around the house, rocking her, talking to her, trying to feed her from a bottle. Exhausted, as the light begins to change outside, she finally goes into the garden and sits cross-legged underneath a large tree, surrounded by her flowers and plants.

Her head tilts as she rocks the baby with her knee like an Indian ayah would. Up and down she rocks the baby in rhythmic motion, (Malayalam) words, phrases from a song, coming out of her mouth.

LILY
(singing)

Nee nee baba nee nee . . .

As Lily sings and sings, the baby finally stops crying. She begins to open her eyes, her tiny hands reach up towards her mother's face, her head bends forward as Lily puts the baby to her breast.

86 EXT. WELLINGTON HOSPITAL—DAY

A group of nurses stand near Mary. We hear them whispering and see them in their white uniforms, walking towards the bench. Mary lies across the bench, moaning and rocking an imaginary 'Baba'.

128

NURSE 1

Are you sure it's her?

NURSE 2

Yes, of course it's her. She looks like a madwoman.

NURSE 1

She's been there all night.

NURSE 2

She must have been sacked.

NURSE 1

Shame! She had a chance.

MARY
(crying)

Baba . . . Baba . . .

87 EXT. ALMS HOUSE—ROAD—DAY

A long empty stretch of road near the docks. Mary is sitting on the road across from an old abandoned ship. She leans down, her face is dirty. She is weary and Lily's dress is even more stained and tattered, like that of a homeless woman. She still wears the red scarf around her head.

After a while, a girl (Mira—from the Alms house) walks along the opposite side of the road. She's holding a bottle of orange pop with a straw. Mary calls out to her and beckons.

MARY

Come here . . . Come here . . .

Mira crosses over to her, recognizing her. She looks at Mary, curious and concerned, but a little afraid. Mary motions to her throat.

MARY

Give me a sip darling, my throat is so dry.

Mary pulls out the straw, then takes several deep gulps from the bottle. The girl watches Mary drink.

MIRA

Take some more.

Mary shakes her head and hands back the bottle.

MARY

Thank you, darling. Thank you my pet. Give me your hand. Help me to get up. My legs are too tired now.

Mira reaches out to help. Mary leans against her as she gets up.

88   INT. ALMS HOUSE—DAY

Mattie winds up a gramophone and dances by herself to the music. We see from the expression on her face and the way she dances that she has danced like this many times before. A clique of women play cards, some still in housecoats and nighties. Shocked, they all turn to stare at Mary, as Mira leads her to the veranda.

WOMEN

What happened? See how filthy she is. Look at her face.

Blossom and Gwen preside. While they talk, Mary sits, now like the other Alms house women, looking out into the street.

GWEN

We could have told her this would happen. No job, who will pay her upkeep and all? How shall I manage all this?

BLOSSOM

She can do some work here, sister. Some cleaning. Something. *(Pause)* Put on a fresh dress, Mary. One of mine will do.

GWEN

Yes, look how dirty she is. she must change from that filthy rag. Mattie will give her a bath. At least we can use it for a dust cloth.

She points inside.

GWEN

She can stay there. Daisy Auntie has passed now, God rest her soul.

Mary looks at a small patch of floor in a corner of the old reading room where women and a few children live, huddled one against another.

A picture of the Queen hangs on the wall.

Mira leads Mary to her spot. She hands her a clean towel, a bar of soap, a lota. An old mat is rolled up against the wall. Mary spreads the mat and lies down.

BLOSSOM
(to ladies in the background)

She wasn't like our church madam. They would never act like this. Ungrateful wretch.

89   EXT. MACINTOSH HOUSE—DAY

The chowkidar and the sweeper girl watch as the driver loads three large suitcases onto the roof of an Ambassador car and ties them down with rope. The chowkidar reaches up to help him.

Theresa stands next to her father and mother, her gaze wandering off into the distance, her hand distractedly pulling the petals off a flower she has just picked. John kneels down next to her.

JOHN

You understand, don't you darling? Daddy has to stay and do some more work for his job but you'll be coming back in just a few months. Mummy's going to write me and tell me all about your new school. You'll see all your old friends again. And then you'll be back before you know it.

THERESA

Will you stay here, at the house?

JOHN

Yes, of course. And all the things in your room will be just where you left them when you come back. Everything will be the same. All right?

He reaches out to hug her, holding her tightly, his eyes filling with tears.

JOHN

And when you come back the baby will be much better and we can all take a long holiday.

LILY

Come on, darling. We don't want to be late.

131

Lily takes her hand and leads her to the car. Theresa sees her mother hesitate in front of the house and then turn quickly to kiss her father. They hurriedly embrace, their faces polite and unresponsive.

LILY

Goodbye, John.

She sees the door closing, feels the cool flat texture of the leather seats, the house slipping away as the car begins to move forward down the gravel road towards the town.

Lily puts her arm around Theresa, drawing her next to her. She motions to the window. Just then the car turns onto a big road and the landscape changes; groves of coconut trees turn to a profusion of green, thick leafy cashew nut trees and banana trees bend against an old stone wall which leads to an open stretch of sea.

90   EXT. ALMS HOUSE—DAY

Subdued, Mary sits on the veranda like all the other Alms house ladies, wearing a plain cotton shift, her hair in two plaits. She watches Mira leaning against the railings of the veranda, smiling to someone down below. Her skirt lifts in the breeze. Mary beckons, her energy lifting as if she recognizes something in her.

MARY

Come. Come here.

MIRA

Yes, Auntie?

MARY

You mustn't stand like that. You want to look like a village girl? See what happened to Dorothy DeCosta's child. They'll give you one wallup and you'll be out.

Mira looks at Mary, curious, impressed.

MARY

Sit down. Sit and pray with me. Our Father who Art in heaven, hallowed be Thy name . . .

Mira repeats the prayer, but her eyes wander.

MIRA

Madam had a nice house, Mary? Was it a big house?

Mary hesitates.

Keep your mind on the job, child. How will you ever leave this place? You must keep your mind on the job.

FADE TO BLACK

THE END

UNIVERSAL PICTURES PRESENT
A MERCHANT IVORY PRODUCTION
COTTON MARY

Directed by
Ismail Merchant

Written by
Alexandra Viets

Produced by
Nayeem Hafizka
Richard Hawley

Music
Richard Robbins

Photography
Pierre Lhomme

Co-Director
Madhur Jaffrey

Executive Producer
Paul Bradley

Production Designer
Alison Riva

Editor
John David Allen

Costumes
Sheena Napier

Associate Costume Designer
Shahnaz Vahanvaty

Sound
Giovanni Di Simone

Associate Producers
Rahila Bootwala
Gil Donaldson

Additional Music
L. Subramaniam

Casting
Celestia Fox

A FILM BY ISMAIL MERCHANT

CAST IN ORDER OF APPEARANCE

Cotton Mary	Madhur Jaffrey
Rosie	Sakina Jaffrey
Abraham	Prayag Raj
Lily Macintosh	Greta Scacchi
Theresa	Laura Lumley
Baba	Matteo Piero Mantegazza
	Olivia Caesar
Mugs	Riju Bajaj
Nurse 1	Cuckoo Parameswaran
Nurse 2	Beena Manoj
Nurse 3	Maggie Arthasery
Doctor Correa	Gerson Da Cunha
Matron	Mahabanoo Mody-Kotwal
John Macintosh	James Wilby
Blossom	Neena Gupta
Gwen	Surekha Sikri
Mattie	Nadira
Mira	Harshiya Rafiq
Guitar Player	Vinnie D'Souza
Inspector Ramji Raj	Captain Raju
Tea Worker 1	Chinappa
Tea Worker 2	Ashok Koshy
Mrs Davids	Gemma Jones
Mrs Smythe	Joanna David
Mrs Evans	Sarah Badel
Mr Panamal	Firdausi Jussawalla
Ayah 1	Shirly Somasundram
Ayah 2	Shobha Vijay
Ayah 3	Jaya George
Jack	Philip Tabor
Charlie	Luke Jones
Bunny Rogers	Susan Malick

Fisherman	Hamza
Joseph	Virendra Saxena
Receptionist	Poornima Mohan
Stylist	Caroline Charlety
Stylist	Ranjini Haridas
Stylist	Gayatri Krishnan
Sylvie D'Costa	Txuku Iriarte Solana
First Assistant Director	Simon V. Kurian
Third Assistant Directors	Luke Jones
	Rizwan Chowhan
	Suraj Varma
Production Manager	John Scholz
Production Controller	Sunil Kirparam
Production Cashier	Toufique Baig
Production Co-ordinator (India)	Jayalakshmy Ramachandran
Production Co-ordinator (UK)	Gillean Dickie
Production Co-ordinator (New York)	Marla Shelton
Key Production Assistant	Amitabh Ghosh
Production Assistants	Siraj Bharapurwala
	Vinaya Chandran
	Caroline Charlety
	P.J. Josey
	Karim Kazi
	Faiza Khan
	Mahadev Mhaske
	V.P. Sajimon
Camera Operator	Jake Polonsky
First Camera Assistant	Jean Pierre Supe
Second Camera Assistant	Vishnu Rao
Third Camera Assistant	Raj Rikhi

Gaffer	Pierre Abraham
Best Boy/A.C.	Gyanchand Rikhi
Key Grip	Manilal Waghela
Dolly Grip	Giri Anchan
Electric/Grips	Rambali Mishra
	Janardhan Rumde
	Maqsood Ali
	Mukesh Waghela
	Sanjay Mishra
	Bhagwat Satkar
	Maruti Thakur
	A. Natarajan
	Enbadas
Boom Operator	Steven Sollars
Sound Trainee	Jamie Graham
Art Director	Charmian Adams
Co-Art Director/	
Construction Manager	Suresh Sawant
Art Department Assistant	Rony Thomas
Property Buyers	Deborah Wilson (England)
	Barbara Herman-Skelding (England)
	Shahji (India)
Property Master	Amar Dogra
Property Assistant	Joseph Nellickal
Standby Props	Mandar Karmarkar
Carpenters	Ashok Panchal
	Gajanand Panchal
	Sadanand Bhikaji
	Anant Ladge
	Ashok Raut
	Abdul Vaid
	Satya Narayan
Painters	Dinkar Sawant
	R.D. Pawar

Construction Assistant	Balkrishna Palkar
Assistant Costume Designer	Flora Avery
Wardrobe Mistress	Urmilla Lal Motwani
Wardrobe Man	Ravi Pawar
Tailor	Abdul Jabbar
Key Make-up & Hair Design	Martina Kohl
Additional Make-up & Hair	Lori Baker
Assistant Hairdresser	Alexis Fernandes
Script Supervisor	Zoe Morgan
Stills Photographer	Seth Rubin
Associate Editors	Jack Tucker A.C.E.
	Giorgio De Vincenzo
Assistant Editor	Paul Clegg
Supervising Sound Editor	Nigel Mills
Dialogue Editor	Nina Hartstone
ADR Editor	Robert Ireland
Foley Editors	Peter Holt
	Robin Quinn
Foley/ADR Mixer	Kevin Tayler
Sound Assistant	Natalie Bayford
Re-recording Mixers	John Hayward
	Richard Pryke
Music Arranger	Geoffrey Alexander
Conductor	Harry Rabinowitz
Music Engineer	Kirsty Whalley
Assistant Music Engineer	Nick Harris

Music recorded at C.T.S. Studios, London
Filmed on location in Kerala, India
© 1999 Cotton Productions